CONTENTS

EPHESIANS

The Glory of the Church

by

Homer A. Kent, Jr.

MOODY PRESS
CHICAGO

To
BECKY, my firstborn
with deep affection and the earnest prayer
that she, like the Ephesians, may know increasingly
"the love of Christ which passeth knowledge."

© 1971 by
THE MOODY BIBLE INSTITUTE
OF CHICAGO

ISBN: 0-8024-2049-4

NOTE: The author has translated Ephesians from the original Greek and has employed this translation in his commentary.

13 14 15 16 17 Printing/LC/Year 88 87 86 85 84

Library of Congress Catalog Number: 77-155689

Printed in the United States of America

INTRODUCTION

EPHESUS, one of the largest cities in the Mediterranean world during New Testament times, had its share of great preachers. Its one-quarter to one-half million population was first touched with the gospel by Paul on his second missionary journey. Later its Christians thrilled to the preaching of the eloquent Apollos. Paul himself devoted three years on his third missionary journey to the proclamation of the gospel in Ephesus and to the instruction of the saints. In succeeding years Timothy ministered there in Paul's stead. Toward the close of the first century, John, the last surviving apostle, made Ephesus his base of operations.

Eventually, however, the voices of these incomparable men were stilled. The people to whom they directed their labors lived out their lives and passed away. Even Ephesus itself became deserted, and only in modern times have its ruins been uncovered by the archeologist's shovel. Yet the name of Ephesus has continued, not because of its pagan temple or its past glories, but chiefly because its Christians were the recipients of a letter from the apostle Paul. The voices of its great preachers died away, but the epistle to the Ephesians lives on and continues to bring its message to a grateful church.

AUTHOR

That the epistle to the Ephesians was written by the apostle Paul is claimed by the opening words of the letter and has been the prevailing view of the church throughout her history. Modern doubt has raised questions about the number of words employed which are not found in other Pauline writings, as well as the presence of certain expressions not characteristically Pauline. Neither of these issues argues conclusively against Paul's authorship, and the traditional view is still the one most widely held.

ADDRESSEES

A greater problem centers around the destination of the epistle. The phrase "at Ephesus" (1:1) appears in the vast majority of ancient manuscripts but is missing from such highly rated texts as codices Sinaiticus and Vaticanus (4th century) and papyrus 46 (3d century). Even these, however, list the title of the epistle as "To the Ephesians." Certain of the early Christian writers (Tertullian, Origen, Basil) discussed the problem, but did not fully settle it.

It is also to be noted that the letter contains no clear references to Paul's experiences in Ephesus, and no greetings sent to anyone by name. Furthermore, such statements as those in 1:15 and 3:2 are sometimes thought to be difficult to harmonize with the idea that Paul was writing to a church well known to him. It has been proposed that this epistle may be the "letter to the Laodiceans" referred to in Colossians 4:16.

Probably the most popular explanation of the missing words is to regard the epistle as an encyclical letter to churches geographically near Ephesus. A space was supposedly left in the manuscript for each church's name to be inserted. Some such expedient seems warranted because the mere omission of "at Ephesus" leaves a most awkward construction in the Greek text. "The saints who are" is not likely to have been the full extent of Paul's original statement. The fact that the reading "at Ephesus" has survived in the bulk of manuscripts is due to the fact that Ephesus was the largest city and presumably had the most influential church. Thus its copy of the letter became the parent for most other copies that were made in succeeding years.

This explanation is not without its weaknesses. When Paul wrote a circular letter to the churches of Galatia, he left no blank space for the church names to be inserted. Nor did such circular letters as the Petrine epistles or 1 John follow such a pattern. There actually are no insurmountable reasons against our understanding that the epistle was originally sent to Ephesus. So reads the text in the vast majority of manuscripts. Lack of references to individuals is characteristic of Paul when writing to churches well known to him. His longest lists of names are in letters where he does not know the congregation as a whole (cf. Ro; Col). To overcome the barrier of unfamiliarity, he mentions in those letters all the individuals he does know. But in churches where all the congregation was known by him personally, he generally avoids mentioning names, lest he be thought to show partiality.

CIRCUMSTANCES OF WRITING

Paul wrote Ephesians while he was under house arrest in Rome, awaiting the outcome of his appeal to Caesar. This would place the time between A.D. 59 and 61. The three epistles —Colossians, Philemon, and Ephesians—were all delivered by the same messenger, Tychicus, and apparently on the same journey (Eph 6:21-22; Col 4:7). Hence they were written at approximately the same time. This may account for the many similarities of expression and content in Colossians and Ephesians. Perhaps they were penned on successive days. It must have been near the time when he expected release from imprisonment (Phile 22). A date of A.D. 61 would appear reasonable.

OUTLINE

Part One

GREETING

1:1—2

1

GREETING

1:1-2

THE WRITER (1:1a)

THE DISCOVERY of numerous papyrus letters dating from the same period as the New Testament reveals that the writers of the New Testament epistles followed the same general literary form as their contemporaries, with certain distinctively Christian additions. Letters usually began with the naming of the author and the addressee, followed by a greeting. The epistle to the Ephesians is no exception.

The writer names himself as Paul, the Roman name which he always used in the Gentile world. Because he was the son of a Jew who was also a Roman citizen, and grew up in a Greek-speaking city, he undoubtedly had two names from birth (i.e., Paul and Saul).

Paul claims the position of apostle of Christ Jesus. This statement indicates the official character of the letter. Furthermore, the title reveals that the term *apostle* is used here in the restricted sense of one who was directly chosen by Christ, as distinct from others called "apostles" in the more general sense (e.g., Epaphroditus, who was called "your apostle" because he was chosen by the Philippian church, Phil 2:25, Gk.). The restricted use seems limited to the Twelve and Paul. It should be understood, as in the sense of Ephesians 4:11, as referring to the apostles who were directly chosen by Christ and granted as gifts to the church for its establishment (cf. also Eph 2:20).

Although he wrote while confined as a prisoner in Rome, Paul had no doubt that his ministry was the will of God for him. This conviction sustained him through his trials. Its mention conveys the sense of authority which he felt and may also suggest his own sense of humility. His ministry was not the product of his own choosing, but was God's doing from beginning to end.

THE READERS (1:1b)

The addressees are called saints and believers in Christ Jesus. The original grammar indicates that this forms one grammatical unit. "In Christ Jesus" belongs with the whole phrase. Paul looks at them as in vital union with Christ. As such they are "set-apart ones" (lit. meaning of "saints") by the action of God who saved them. Viewed from the human side, they are believers, ones who have trusted Christ. Thus the description refers to all true believers.

They are residing at Ephesus. (See Introduction for discussion of textual problem.) This city was the scene of Paul's longest ministry recorded in Acts. He first preached in the city on the return portion of his second missionary journey (Ac 18:19-21). On the third missionary journey, he stayed three years (19:1—20:1, 31). Ephesus was the chief city of the Roman province of Asia. It was the site of the great temple of Artemis, which housed the image of the goddess supposedly fallen from heaven. The city's open-air theater could seat twenty-five thousand people. In later years Timothy and the apostle John would have extended ministries in this important city.

THE SALUTATION (1:2)

The classical greeting in Greek letters used an infinitive form (see Ja 1:1; Ac 23:26) which we usually translate simply as "Greetings." In Paul's letters, however, he changes the form slightly to the cognate word *grace* and couples with it the common Jewish greeting "peace." This joining of grace and peace (always in this order in Paul's opening greetings) thus adapts the well-known formulas of the Greek and Hebrew worlds into a most meaningful Christian expression. It indicates Paul's desire that his readers enjoy the favor of God which will produce the inner satisfaction that stabilizes the heart (Phil 4:7).

These blessings find their source in God our Father and Jesus Christ our Lord. The joining of these two persons indicates that both are of equal rank in the mind of the writer.

Part Two

DOCTRINE CONCERNING
THE CHURCH

1:3—3:21

2

AN ASCRIPTION OF PRAISE TO GOD

1:3-14

THIS SECTION CONTAINS one of the most glorious and most symmetrical doxologies to be found in Scripture. It consists of three stanzas, each concluded by the repetition of a phrase (vv. 6, 12, 14), and each emphasizing a different Person of the Trinity. In scope it covers the entire sweep of redemption, from its beginning in the election of God to its consummation in the receiving of our inheritance.

THE FATHER WHO CHOSE US (1:3-6)

The blessings which believing men have received from God prompt their blessing of Him through worship. Paul is thinking specifically of the spiritual blessings from God—those blessings relating to the believer's new nature and position.

These blessings are "in heavenly places." In the original text the phrase is literally "in the heavenlies." Although this adjective is used elsewhere with nouns, only in Ephesians do we find it standing alone, and it occurs this way five times (1:3, 20; 2:6; 3:10; 6:12). Comparison of all these passages indicates its meaning to be the sphere of spiritual blessing in which believers even now participate (1:3; 2:6). In this realm Christ is supreme (1:20). Angelic beings also reside "in the heavenlies" and are observers of God's wisdom as displayed in the church (3:10). Presently, however, even evil spiritual forces exist "in the heavenlies" and confront believers on earth (6:12). Hence Paul means that believers today have a new existence

19

in that realm of spiritual reality where God is the source of life. Spiritual warfare is being waged in this realm today, but when Christ returns to establish His kingdom He will accomplish His will completely, "on earth as it is in heaven."

A more specific statement of the Father's action is given in verse 4. It was He who initiated the plan of redemption by choosing believers in connection with Christ before the foundation of the world. This sovereign act of God chose some to experience the blessings of salvation. The reasons or criteria for His choice have not been told to us, except that it was according to His own good pleasure (1:9). The fact of a chosen group was well known to Jews, from the Old Testament (Deu 4:37; 7:6-8; Is 41:8), but now it is revealed that God's election in the church includes Gentiles also.

This election by God was "in him" (i.e., Christ). God found in Christ the all-sufficient merits for redeeming men without violating His righteousness. His purpose was to secure persons whose lives would demonstrate God's power in overcoming sin. His election was done in love and it engenders love in believers. It is questioned whether justification or sanctification is in view in the latter part of verse 4. Because Paul uses the same Greek words regarding sanctification in 5:27 (trans. "holy and without blemish"), it does not seem advisable to leave out the ethical aspect. Paul views both the judicial and the experiential as being God's purpose in election. (It is possible that the phrase "in love" belongs with verse 5, "in love having predestinated us." However, Paul's usual practice is to place such a phrase after the words it qualifies rather than before.)

The method of God's election is stated in verse 5. The words "having predestinated" are probably modal rather than temporal. Paul is explaining the manner in which election was effected. It was accomplished by God's marking out some for salvation even before their personal existence. This predestination was God's selection of some to receive adoption as His sons.

Roman custom seems to be in the background of the illustration, since there was no comparable Jewish custom. By this practice, boys of other families might be legally adopted and granted full rights and responsibilities. This is precisely what God did when He chose men who because of sin had no spiritual life. By God's choice He made them His sons. Of course, the spiritual truth far outstrips the human illustration, for by regeneration God actually makes such persons His sons by nature through new birth. (See Gal 4:1-7 for a similar illustration by Paul.)

No room is left for human pride, for Gods' election was in no sense dependent on man. It was accomplished "through Jesus Christ," and is to be explained only by "the good pleasure of his will." God's choice was not governed by anything good or attractive in man, nor anything outside of God Himself. It was an act of His own goodness, and beyond this we cannot go.

One should beware of drawing false conclusions from this sublime truth. Paul is not stating a harsh and fatalistic doctrine in which God arbitrarily selects some for heaven, no matter how evil their lives, and consigns others to hell, regardless of how sincerely they may wish to do God's will. On the contrary, the Bible teaches that all men are dead in sin, and none at all would be saved if God did not intervene. Furthermore, Scripture never speaks of men being predestinated for hell. Predestination in the Bible always is in reference to believers. God's matchless plan also provided the means as well as the end. It is still true that "whosoever will may come." And it is due to God's sovereign grace that some do respond in faith and come to God through Christ.

The refrain in verse 6 ends each stanza of this doxology. It shows how each phase of our redemption moves toward the praise and glory of God. In Paul's view, redemption originated solely with God and was made effective by His unchanging decrees. It is the greatest display of grace conceivable, for it bestows the most glorious privileges on completely depraved and fallen men, and this bestowal is all one-sided. Man merely accepts or rejects; he brings no merits.

A more literal rendering of verse 6b would be, "which He freely gave us in the Beloved." This is the only New Testament occurrence of this title for Christ. Yet we are prepared for it by the Father's own words at the baptism and transfiguration, "This is my beloved Son." Paul refers to Christ in Colossians 1:13 as the "Son of his love" (ASV). It is as we are "in" Him, that is, in vital spiritual union with Christ, that our adoption as sons of God becomes the reality which God's gracious election has planned.

CHRIST WHO REDEEMED US (1:7-12)

The second stanza of this incomparable doxology puts emphasis on the function of Christ the Son. Paul mentions two great provisions which Christ supplies: redemption (vv. 7-10) and a heritage (vv. 11-12).

Redemption is first described as to its nature (v. 7). It consists in release from servitude by the payment of a ransom. While it may be true that sometimes the word is used more generally of deliverance, here the inclusion of "through his blood" clearly names the ransom price. Sinners who were enslaved to sin and in hopeless debt to the righteousness of God were redeemed by the blood of Christ. It was not merely His death but the sacrificial nature of that death, as the mention of "blood" signifies.

Redemption accomplished the forgiveness of our transgressions. (See Col 1:14 for a parallel statement.) Redemption was secured at Calvary when the price was paid. Forgiveness becomes experienced when individual men respond in faith to the gospel. The basic idea in forgiveness is remission—the removal of guilt. The apostles were instructed to "remit" sins by proclaiming the gospel (Jn 20:23; Ac 10:42-43). The higher one's conception of God's holiness and the deeper his sense of human sin, the greater is his discernment of the riches of grace that were necessary to provide such a redemption.

The scope of redemption is set forth in verses 8-10. It has been revealed to believers as of stupendous sweep. In Christ, God caused His grace to abound to us in the sphere of all wisdom and intelligence. Although some refer the terms *wisdom* and *prudence* to God, it seems better to understand them as referring to human characteristics which God by His abounding grace has provided to the sinner whereby he can understand and accept what God has done. (Cf. Col 1:9.) The wisdom of which Paul speaks is the general term for intellectual insight which comprehends spiritual truth. Such wisdom comes from above (Ja 1:5; 3:15, 17). Prudence or intelligence is the practical use of wisdom. It is God's abounding grace which enables man to perceive intellectually and to accept and put into practice the provisions of God's redemptive plan.

God multiplied His grace to believing men in revealing to them the mystery of His will—certain aspects of which had not formerly been declared. ("Mystery" in the New Testament does not mean something mysterious, but truth previously concealed and now made known.) What was revealed was His will to provide in Christ the focal point of redemption so that all things might be brought into a grand unity (cf. Col 1:16-20).

The word *dispensation* actually means administration or management. "The fulness of times" is an expression similar to one used to describe the period which began with Christ's first coming (Gal 4:4). It will reach its consummation when Christ comes again. It is called the fullness of the times because it is the period long prophesied in the Old Testament as bringing about the consummation of God's plan through Messiah. Thus we find the New Testament referring to the present age as "the ends of the world" (lit. "ends of the ages," 1 Co 10:11), "last time" (lit. "last hour," 1 Jn 2:18), and "these last days" (Heb 1:2).

Paul, therefore, is stating that now God has revealed to us His plan for the management of the universe. It consists in bringing together all things in Christ. This includes "all things," both in heaven and on earth. Some relate this summation in Christ only to personal salvation or to the church, and thus avoid any sort of universalism. The "all-things" are explained in the light of the election stated in 1:4. The neuter "things," however, seems to imply more than just persons. Also the similar passage in Colossians 1:20 would suggest that Paul has a much wider concept at this point, including angels as well. This does not mean that he is teaching universal salvation either here or in Colossians 1:20, but that he is presenting Christ as the grand unifying factor of all things which we can conceive. God has a plan for the universe and it will be fully accomplished through Christ. By the redemption which He made, sin was defeated and righteousness for man provided. Even the physical universe will eventually be cleansed from the disastrous effects which sin has caused, and all is due to the divine management which God put into operation through Christ.

The second provision by Christ was the believers' constitution as a heritage of God (vv. 11-12). The translation in the American Standard Version—"were made a heritage" (similarly in TEV)—is closer to the original text than "obtained an inheritance" (KJV). The point is that in Christ, God has made believers His own heritage. We are His own people. This is terminology similar to many Old Testament passages in which God's people were called His "inheritance" (Deu 4:20; 9:29; 32:9; etc.).

Now all of this is a part of God's plan. Just as the first stanza grounded salvation in God's sovereign choice, so the second stanza reemphasizes the fact that the redeeming work of Christ is likewise a part of that great plan. Redemption made us a heritage of God, and this was because we have been "predestinated according to the purpose of him who worketh all things after the counsel of his own will." The words *counsel* and *will* are similar in meaning in the Greek language. It is generally agreed, however, that the former connotes deliberation and the latter conveys the more general idea of volition with perhaps the thought of inclination. If so, Paul is saying that predestination is carried out in perfect harmony with the reasons God had regarding His will for men. What these reasons were is not revealed to us. But it is incorrect to say that predestination has no reasons. God has them; we don't happen to know them.

In verse 12 appears the recurring phrase which concludes each stanza of this glorious statement of praise. The redemptive work of Christ made possible the accomplishment of God's elective plan, and was intended ultimately to result in praise of God's glory as lost men are transformed into beings who can fellowship with God for eternity.

"Who first trusted in Christ" is variously explained. Some interpret it of Christians generally, and understand "first" from the future standpoint of verse 14. Christians trust first, and will later experience the consummation of redemption. However, the "ye also" of verse 13 is in contrast to those of verse 12, and thus verse 12 must be naming a restricted group. Others identify those who first trusted as Old Testament Jews whose hope in Messiah (the word *trusted* is better rendered "hoped") began before Christ's arrival. The best explanation, however, is that which refers it to Jewish Christians who were as a group evangelized before the Gentiles. In fact, Gentile evangelization at first had to overcome serious opposition from many Jewish Christians. Here Paul in tracing the plan of redemption from eternity past identifies himself with the chosen nation ("us"), but then goes on in verse 13 to show how God's plan also includes Gentiles on no inferior basis. This view gives proper emphasis to "ye also" of verse 13, and uses the concept of hoping in Christ in the full regenerative sense that this context calls for.

THE HOLY SPIRIT WHO SEALED US (1:13-14)

The final stanza of the doxology mentions the function of the Holy Spirit, who also has a vital part in making the Father's plan effective. The Father devised the plan and chose us. Christ set the plan in operation by shedding His blood for our redemption. The Holy Spirit causes men to be united to Christ and thus to become participants in the plan of redemption.

Paul first names two actions of the believers which were a preparation for the Spirit's sealing ministry. They first heard the word of truth. This was the gospel—God's message of good news which revealed to man that Christ died for sin, and He offers complete forgiveness and eternal life to those who will believe. Then they had believed the message and had come to experience salvation. (KJV supplies the verb "trusted" after "ye also" in v. 13. It is better, however, to supply nothing, but to understand "ye also" as the subject of "were sealed," with the intervening words being a not uncommon explanatory digression by Paul.)

He then explains the effect which God produces. Believers are sealed with the Holy Spirit. This sealing is mentioned two other times in the New Testament (2 Co 1:22; Eph 4:30). Sealing suggests safekeeping, ownership, authentication, and sometimes secrecy. The last is hardly in view here, but the other connotations may all have been in the writer's mind. We are not to suppose that the sealing of the Holy Spirit is some experience subsequent to salvation or is the possession of only some believers. Paul states that these same Ephesians who had heard and believed had also been sealed. The implication is that all of them had. Furthermore, "after that ye believed" is a participle in the Greek text which here names coincident action and may therefore be translated "when ye believed." By calling the Spirit "the Holy Spirit of promise," he refers to the fact that Christ had promised to the disciples that He would send the Spirit, a promise that was fulfilled at Pentecost (Ac 1:5; 2:33, 38) and is shared by all subsequent believers at conversion (Ac 10:44-47; 11:15-17).

The coming of the Spirit to each believer provides the earnest of his inheritance. An earnest is a down payment which assures the seller of the good faith of the purchaser and of the eventual payment in full. Thus the indwelling Holy Spirit whom all believers now possess is an assurance and a foretaste of what shall be full salvation (see also 2 Co 5:5).

The goal of this sealing is stated as twofold. It guarantees the eventual experiencing of all aspects of redemption. Believers themselves are God's purchased possession. What we now enjoy in part will ultimately be experienced to the full (cf. Ro 8:15-24). There is also a benefit which God receives. By the work of the Spirit in regenerating and sealing believers, praise will come to the Father for all eternity because of His matchless saving grace.

3

PAUL'S FIRST PRAYER FOR HIS READERS

1:15-23

As PAUL has contemplated God's great plan of redemption, he is moved to recognize how it has operated in the lives of his readers and he thanks God for it.

OCCASION (1:15-16)

This prayer was prompted by reports which Paul had received of the faith and love manifested by his readers. Although he uses the expression "having heard" (lit.) of the Colossians whom he had not previously seen (Col 1:4), he also uses it of Philemon whom he did know (Phile 4-5). Thus it is no argument against an Ephesian readership. When it is remembered that Paul had been away from Ephesus for five years, the expression is a natural one. He refers to their progress in faith, as well as to new converts who had been made. "I also" means "I, as well as others, have heard."

Therefore, on the occasions when he prayed, he made mention of the Ephesians. Because of the nature of the reports he had received, he was always able to thank God for their spiritual progress. He was grateful to God that his labors among them were still bearing fruit, as their initial faith in Christ was producing lives of faith, and their Christian vitality was expressing itself properly in love toward one another.

REQUEST (1:17-23)

A general statement is first made, indicating the nature of the prayer. It is a request that the Ephesians may be granted a fuller knowledge of God (1:17). When Paul speaks of the Father as "God of our Lord Jesus Christ," he is echoing the words of Jesus Himself who during His earthly career said, "My God, my God, why hast thou forsaken me?" (Mt 27:46), and "My God, and your God" (Jn 20:17). In His humanity Christ did not hesitate to acknowledge the Father as God.

Paul prays that God may grant his readers the "Spirit of wisdom and revelation." Whether "Spirit" refers to the Holy Spirit, and should be capitalized, or refers to the human spirit, and should be lowercased, is debated by many. Because of the presence of the word *revelation,* it seems better to understand the Holy Spirit here. A person could have a "spirit of wisdom" (i.e., a wise spirit), but how could he possess a "spirit of revelation"? Paul does not mean that believers are to do any revealing, but are to be the recipients of revelation. He wants the Ephesians to be given a deeper understanding of God and His program, and it will be the function of the Holy Spirit to provide this. The term employed for "knowledge" is one which implies a precise and thorough understanding. Spiritual gifts are intended to provide men with a better acquaintance of God, His person, and His plans.

A more detailed description is next given of the content of Paul's prayer. It involved three specific requests. First, he desired his readers to know what was the hope of God's calling (1:18a). To have such an awareness, it was absolutely imperative that they be spiritually enlightened in their hearts. ("Heart" in Scripture refers to the essential part of man's being, particularly the rational, spiritual, and emotional elements.) This had occurred at regeneration (the perfect participle "having been enlightened" denotes the present condition resulting from a past act). Full knowledge is not merely a set of theological propositions to be learned, but is an ever growing experience of the truth about God.

The Ephesians (and all other Christians) needed a deeper appreciation of the hope which was included in the call of God to which they had responded. This hope was objective in that it provided certain future realities as the believer's prospect, and it was also subjective in that it created in each believer an attitude of trust and hopefulness as he anticipates these future glories.

Paul also asked for them a greater awareness of the riches of the glory of the inheritance which God has prepared for bestowal among the saints (1:18b). This petition looks forward to the time when faith will become sight and hope shall be realized.

The third petition desired that the Ephesians might get to know more fully the greatness of God's power in relation to believers (1:19-23). This divine energy is described as the "working" of God's strength. This term always depicts energy in operation. Of its eight New Testament occurrences, all are used of supernatural power, either of God (six times) or Satan (twice). Paul does not let the power of God remain as a theological abstraction. The great measure and illustration of God's effective power is the resurrection of Christ. Paul wants his readers to see that this very power is operating in them. How great this power is may be seen in considering the uniqueness of the resurrection event. No one else ever produced a true resurrection. (All previous raisings may be regarded almost as resuscitations, because they were merely a return to mortal life followed ultimately by physical death again.)

The power of God not only raised Jesus from the dead but also elevated Him to the Father's right hand, the place of authority as well as honor. In this exaltation Christ resumed the prerogatives which He had voluntarily laid aside during His earthly ministry. (On earth Christ exercised these powers under the guidance of the Father and the Spirit only to the degree that they were needed for His redemptive work.) "In the heavenlies" (see on 1:3) is the second occurrence of this phrase in Ephesians. Here the concept of locality is prominent. Heaven is the seat of divine authority over the spiritual sphere.

The exaltation of Christ by the Father elevated Him far above all other entities. From similar enumerations in Romans 8:38, Ephesians 3:10, Colossians 1:16, and 1 Peter 3:22, it seems clear that Paul is referring to various orders of angelic beings. The context in each of these passages makes it unlikely that any sort of human government is in view. However, the varied order in which these lists appear prevents our making any arbitrary decisions as to lower and higher rank. "Every name that is named" reminds one of Philippians 2:9, where Christ is said to be given the "name which is above every name." Regardless of how men may speculate about the angelic world, and the degree of rank and prestige possessed by angels, and no matter what dignified name men may bestow upon them, Christ is above them all. This fact holds true not only for the present age in which men live, but also for that Messianic age to come and the eternal state into which it merges. In both these vast ages, angels will continue to exist (and doubtless in orderly ranks), but Christ will always be superior to them.

In Christ's exaltation, all creation has been subjected to Him (Ps 8:6). This one whom the Father has established as head over the angelic realm and all the rest of creation as well has been given to the church as its head also. The exact relation of Christ to the church is next developed. This is the major emphasis of the epistle and is elaborated in succeeding chapters.

The power of God has constituted the church as a living organism—a body with Christ as its head. Christ is thus not merely the leader (who conceivably might be replaced through some reorganization), but is indissolubly connected to the church as a head is to its body.

The church as the body of Christ is also described as "the fulness of him that filleth." The point is probably not that the church is that which makes Christ complete, for such is hardly the thought Paul is developing in this passage. Rather, Paul means that the church as Christ's body is filled by Him with all the graces and powers which it possesses. The same thought is expressed in John 1:16, Ephesians 3:19 and Colossians 2:10. It is Christ who Himself possesses all the fullness of God (Col 1:19; 2:9), and who provides believers with all of the powers they need. The prayer closes with a sweeping reminder of the magnificence of Christ. He is the one who fills all the universe with all that it contains and needs. It is this same Christ who is the great supplier for the church of all its needs.

Frequently in Paul's career, he had to combat wrong teaching which diverted men from trusting solely in Christ. Some insisted on veneration of angels (Col 2:18), others on religious observances (Gal 5:1-2). Ascetic practices (Col 2:20-23), human philosophies (Col 2:8), and unworthy human leaders (2 Ti 2:17-18) all had their devotees. The epistle to the Ephesians sounds the note with unmistakable clarity that Christ is the head of the church, and as its head He supplies it with all the fullness of divine life and power. This inexhaustible power of God, displayed to us in Christ, is what Paul prays here that believers should come to know.

4

REGENERATION OF BELIEVERS

2:1-10

THEIR FORMER CONDITION (2:1-3)

HAVING LAID an appropriate foundation by relating God's plan of salvation and His mighty power which effected it through Christ, Paul now explains how this was made operative in the lives of the Ephesians.

God had saved them, not because of their goodness, but at a time when they were "dead in trespasses and sins." They were not merely ailing or undeveloped, but were completely unresponsive to God and His righteousness. Spiritually they were dead and in need of resurrection. No program of reform would do. They needed new life.

It should be noted that Paul begins the sentence with the object, and the verb does not occur until verse 5 ("he made alive"). Because of the great distance between the two, the King James Version has supplied a verb in verse 1, drawing it, of course, from verse 5. Many have felt that Paul was speaking of Gentile Christians in his reference to "you" (2:1) and then includes Jewish Christians in "also we all" (2:3). However, inasmuch as the verb which governs verse 1 is "made alive" in verse 5 (KJV, "hath quickened"), and the object found in verse 1—"you being dead in trespasses and sins"—is repeated in verse 5 as "we were dead in trespasses," it is doubtful whether Paul has such a sharp distinction in view. In all likelihood he has begun by referring to his readers (both Jewish and Gentile Christians in the church at Ephesus), and then enlarges the reference to include himself and all believers. This is not uncharacteristic of Paul.

Trespasses connote acts which deviate from God's revealed standard. "Sins" translates a term which may look at man's life as missing the goal and thus coming short of what God expects (Ro 3:23). The words here name the instrument through which their spiritually dead condition was effected. They had been dead because of sin. All were sinners by habit as well as by nature.

Their habitual behavior ("walked") had been characterized by sinning. Their standard of conduct had been "according to the age of this world system." Because they were dead toward God, their activity was entirely a response to this world system. They breathed its atmosphere and patterned their lives after it.

What makes such conduct so reprehensible is the fact that it is really a response to Satan, called here (2:2) the prince of the power of the air. The meaning of "air" in all other New Testament passages is literal, but the sense of it here is more difficult. However, there is no strong reason why the simplest understanding of the term as the space above the earth and below heaven cannot be meant. These evil demonic powers move about freely under Satan's control and have access to men on earth as well as to the heavenly region (Job 1:6-7; Eph 6:12).

In the King James Version "The spirit that now worketh" appears as an appositive with "prince," and thus as a further description of Satan. The Greek text, however, forbids such an identification. It is possible grammatically to understand "spirit" as in apposition with "power." Thus Satan is said to be the leader of the evil spiritual power operating today, namely the spirit which energizes all sinful men. When we speak of "the spirit of the age," we are using the word *spirit* in this sense.

It was among the sons of disobedience that all Christians formerly lived their lives. It made no difference whether they were Gentiles or Jews, or whether they resided in Ephesus or were part of an apostolic mission; all formerly lived their lives ("had our conversation" is an old English way of saying this) by yielding to the same impulses and were equally dead before God. Every man apart from God's regenerating work is engaged in carrying out the sinful wishes of his natural self through sinful acts. "Flesh" is used frequently by Paul as a reference to what man is as inherited from Adam. Thus sins of the flesh are not limited to indulgence in the more crude and sensual vices, but also include such evils as strife and envy (see Gal 5:19-21 for one list of sins of the flesh). In this passage it is doubly clear that more than physical flesh is in view, because Paul mentions the mind specifically (the Gk word is plural, and should be understood as "thoughts"). Man apart from God's saving grace has even his rational faculties deranged spiritually. Thoughts can be sinful as well as deeds.

All of this has constituted man as an object of God's wrath. The fact that all men without exception commit sin is evidence of the deeper fact that they share a sinful nature. Our common expression to excuse sin—"It's just human nature"—testifies to this fact. Because the substance of our being was inherited from Adam, the fallen nature which Adam acquired was passed on to all of his descendants. Thus *by nature* all men are abiding under God's holy wrath against sin (Jn 3:36). This was just as true of those who subsequently became believers as of others who remain unbelievers.

THEIR PRESENT STATE

In glorious contrast, Paul points to the only solution to man's spiritual incapacity. "But God" strikes just the right note, for it points to the only conceivable answer to man's need, and yet to the most unlikely answer. After all, it was God whose righteousness had been offended, against whom man had sinned, and whose wrath was now poised against the sinner. From God, man had reason to expect nothing but judgment. Yet if there was to be any hope, God Himself must initiate it, and this is precisely what Paul explains.

God acted out of the riches of His mercy. Nothing whatsoever in man provided the cause or impulse for redemption. Its basis was entirely God's mercy. Furthermore, this attitude of mercy was not a grudging act of charity or a reluctant benefaction but was prompted by God's great love (see Jn 3:16). Redemption thus was not merely an act of sparing sinners from doom (which is what mercy alone might imply) but is rooted in God's matchless love for men whom He created.

This love of God is all the more amazing when we recognize that it was put into operation "even when we were dead in sins" (cf. 2:1). Nothing in us made us worthy or attractive, God's love stood in the starkest contrast to sinners whom He loved. Men were dead spiritually, being without any favorable response to God and incapable in themselves of rectifying their condition. Yet even in such unlikely circumstances, our merciful and loving God intervened.

God's love was brought to bear upon sinners when He "quickened us together with Christ." It was not love in the abstract, nor a sentimentality which paid no heed to what is right or holy. Rather, God's love made us alive (lit. meaning of "quickened") by His identification of believing sinners with His Son. In this way God's righteousness was satisfied by the payment of sin's penalty through the voluntary sacrifice of Christ, whose personal sinlessness and the uniqueness of His person made His death of infinite atoning value as the substitute for sinners.

At the cross, Jesus Christ suffered both physical and spiritual death (i.e., separation of body and soul, and separation of His spirit from the Father for a time), thus experiencing the penalty that God had pronounced upon sinners. When Christ was made alive historically, in the mind of God believers were viewed as in vital union with Christ, and thus new life (regeneration) was achieved. This becomes realized by the believer at the moment of faith.

At this point Paul breaks in with the exclamation, "By grace ye are saved!" How true this is! Only the infinite grace of God could accomplish salvation for sinners, who by definition are spiritually dead. It is God's favor, unmerited by men in any sense, which is solely responsible for salvation. The verb "are saved" (KJV) is sometimes rendered "have been saved" (ASV). Its form depicts a present state resultant from a past action. Paul is saying that believers were saved by the regeneration of God in Christ, and that action resulted in a settled condition which believers now enjoy.

The believer's union with Christ in His resurrection involves him also in the exalted standing which Christ has. Our Lord ascended to the Father and is presently seated in the place of honor and authority. "In the heavenlies" is the third of five occurrences of this expression in Ephesians (see 1:3; 1:20; 3:10; 6:12). Although locality is prominent in the thought here, the other uses indicate that the idea of spiritual sphere is also basic to Paul's thought. In the spiritual sphere where Christ is supreme, believers are also established through union with Him. Of course, although it is evident that the full exercise of these prerogatives must await Christ's coming (even Christ Himself does not yet have all enemies put under His feet, Ac 2:34-35; 3:20-21), the spiritual realities have been accomplished.

Spiritual resurrection (i.e., regeneration) is the subject of this passage. However, it should be observed that this is not unrelated to physical resurrection. One is the consequence of the other. Just as physical death is the inevitable consequence of spiritual death (Adam died spiritually on the very day he sinned, and physical death followed later, Gen 3:7), so spiritual resurrection insures physical resurrection in due time.

THEIR FUTURE PROSPECT (2:7)

Paul's gaze now turns from the present status of believers to the culmination which God has planned for them. "Ages to come" is a reference to the eternal ages which shall be ushered in at Christ's return. At that time, and for all eternity to follow, God's plan of redemption, and the faith exercised in receiving it, will be fully vindicated. The faith will become sight, and the full glories of salvation will be displayed.

This future display will demonstrate clearly the "exceeding riches" of God's grace. The wealth of God's provision has been mentioned in verse 4. Now Paul's point involves the idea that it will take the unending ages of eternity itself to display adequately the opulence of God's grace. Such grace toward sinners is inexhaustible and infinite. It can never be fully revealed to finite creatures in an instant. Both men and angels will marvel throughout eternity at what God has done.

In the context, God's grace has been described as mercy and love (2:4). Now the word *kindness* is added to show the sweet benignity with which God's blessings have been bestowed. His favor has withheld what was due and has relieved the affliction (i.e., mercy). It was not done coldly or condescendingly but in love. And even the way in which He did it showed the utmost graciousness as He elevated believers to a position in union with His Son (surely the greatest "kindness").

EXPLANATION (2:8-10)

What follows is a summary of the previous material with some further explanation. Again (as in 2:5, 7) Paul reminds his readers that they have been saved by God's grace. Actually he says "the grace" in 2:8, meaning that particular grace of God which has been under discussion in the passage. "Are saved" is the same form as in 2:5, depicting the present state resultant from a past action. Here he also adds the expression "through faith," to name the channel through which man receives the salvation God provides. It must not be supposed, however, that faith is in any sense causative. Salvation is not a cooperative venture in which both God and man contribute their parts. It is entirely God's work. Man either receives it or rejects it. "Faith" names the response of those who receive it.

"And this not of yourselves" emphasizes this truth that salvation is in no sense man's work. Some refer "this" to the faith just mentioned, and understand Paul to say that even the faith of the believer is not man's work, but must be produced by God. Against this, however, is the lack of grammatical agreement between "this" (neuter gender) and "faith" (feminine gender in Gk). The same objection applies to "grace" as a possible antecedent. A better explanation understands the neuter "this" as referring to the whole fact contained in the previous statement: salvation by grace through faith. This conserves the idea that even faith is not ultimately the work of man (any more than grace or salvation), but occurs only when God moves upon the heart to bring conviction and then trust.

Salvation is the gift of God from beginning to end, from planning to accomplishment. When Paul says it is "not of works" (2:9), he is giving a further elaboration of "not of yourselves" (v. 8). Not even deeds of righteousness can effect salvation. There can never be the slightest reason for man's personal glorying. Faith is the very opposite of works, for it offers no works to God but rather accepts that work of redemption that God has done. Thus Paul wrote in Romans 3:27 that God's plan of providing salvation through faith excludes all human boasting, for man has contributed nothing to it. Because fallen human nature is so prone to boast of its accomplishments and to take credit where there is even the slightest occasion, God devised a plan to save men in their hopelessness which allows no grounds whatever for human pride to operate.

The emphasis in verse 10 suggests the translation: "For His workmanship are we" ("His" is the first word in the Greek sentence). That is why there is no room for human boasting before God. Even the good works which follow the believer's regeneration are the product of God's Spirit and are no cause for human pride. By calling us God's "workmanship," Paul implies more than appointment. He means that we have been created by Him through new birth. Thus whatever good works may follow our regeneration are still the result of the one who made us.

Now this is not to disparage a life of godliness. On the contrary, God expects believers to perform good works as the fruit of their new life. Verse 10 says regarding good works, "which God hath before ordained that we should walk in them." We note that it does not say that believers were previously prepared to walk in good works, but that the good works were previously prepared that believers might walk in them. Paul's thought is that the Christian is completely without grounds for boasting even in the good works which follow regeneration, for they too are God's handiwork. It was God who long ago planned the good works He wanted us to perform. Our responsibility is to follow His blueprint for our lives, responding to the impulses of His Spirit as He prompts us to perform His will.

5

INCLUSION OF THE GENTILES

2:11-22

THIS SECTION CONTAINS some of the most basic material in the letter, as it describes the church as composed of Gentiles on an equal footing with Jews.

THE GENTILES' PREVIOUS CONDITION (2:11-12)

THEIR IDENTITY (2:11)

In the previous portion of the chapter Paul has discussed the former unsaved condition of his readers in terms common to both Jew and Gentile. Before conversion, all were dead in sins and needed the regenerating work of God. Now Paul looks at the two groups separately and shows what has happened to their distinctions. He asks his readers to remember what they were, as a prelude to proper appreciation of what they have become.

Paul calls his readers "Gentiles in the flesh." The bulk of the Ephesian church must have been Gentiles. They were so "in the flesh" because they did not bear in their bodies the physical sign of circumcision. Such people were commonly called Uncircumcision as a term of reproach by pious Jews who gloried in their traditions and wore the name Circumcision proudly. By describing this circumcision as made by hands, the writer makes it clear that physical circumcision is meant. There is a spiritual "circumcision" which all Christians possess in regeneration (Col 2:11), but that is not the point here.

THEIR DESCRIPTION (2:12)

Five characteristics are noted by the writer. First, they were without Christ. They were not only unsaved, but as Gentiles they were without any Messianic hope for the future. (The Gk name "Christ" is a translation of the Hebrew title "Messiah.") Second, they were alienated from the commonwealth of Israel. Being Gentiles, they had no association with the nation of Israel, a nation which God had chosen to preserve His revelation. It was within this nation that the people of God were to be found at that time, but Gentiles (except for proselytes) were foreigners and thus excluded.

Third, they were strangers from the covenants of promise. This has reference to the promises made to Abraham and his seed, and confirmed at various times to the patriarchs (Gen 12:1-3; 13:15-16; 15:1-6; 17:6-8). As pagan Gentiles in Ephesus, these people formerly had no share in the promises to Abraham, Isaac, and Jacob. The covenant with Abraham did involve future blessing for all the families of the earth, but the covenant was a promise to Abraham and his descendants.

Fourth, they were enjoying no hope. The absence of any article with "hope" indicates that they were not only devoid of "the hope" of salvation in Christ, but were without the very quality of hope for the future. Their lives had been characterized by concentration upon the present world, with no real confidence about the future, whether pertaining to this life or the next. Fifth, they were without God in the world. Paul probably does not mean that they had been atheists in the philosophical sense of acknowledging no gods at all, but that they were ignorant of the true God, regardless of what sort of religious activity they may have pursued. As Gentiles, their previous state is shown to have been utterly bleak and completely devoid of any prospect for God apart from the intervention of God.

THE GENTILES' PRESENT STATUS (2:13)

In contrast to "at that time" (2:12), Gentiles "now" have a

new position. Once far off from salvation, without Christ, without the Old Testament promises, and without God, they now have been made "near" to God. Similar terminology is found in Isaiah 57:19. It was accomplished "in Christ Jesus," and specifically by the "blood of Christ." Blood suggests the sacrificial nature of Christ's death. It was not just His expiration, but the sacrificial shedding of His blood that brought salvation. Hence Gentiles may now enjoy salvation just as Jews, on the basis of the work of Christ at Calvary, made available by God to those who by faith are in vital union with His Son ("in Christ Jesus").

At this point, however, difficulties arose early in the Christian movement. The first Christians were Jews, and they were slow to realize the full implications of Gentile salvation. The idea of Gentiles being saved was not a new one to them, but it was generally assumed that this would be through the avenue of proselytization, just as Gentiles adopted Judaism in former times. Even Peter, who preached of salvation for Gentiles on the day of Pentecost (Ac 2:39), did not understand that this meant Gentiles could be saved *as Gentiles* without first adopting circumcision and other Jewish practices, until God showed him by special revelation (10:28, 34-35). To this problem the next portion of Paul's explanation is directed.

THE JOINING OF GENTILES AND JEWS (2:14-22)

THE MAKING OF ONE BODY (2:14-18)

A literal translation of verse 14 begins, "For He Himself is our peace." The emphatic use of "He" shows that it is Christ and no other. To say Christ "is" our peace, rather than "achieved" our peace stresses the truth that it is Christ in His own person who embodies our peace with God, and between Jew and Gentile. It was He who by the sacrifice of Himself satisfied fully the righteousness of God and made possible the condition of peace instead of wrath.

The emphasis here is on the new unity created between Gentiles and Jews. By making both one, it is not Paul's meaning that Gentiles have become Jews, nor have Jews become Gentiles, but in Christ both have become one with the old distinctions removed. Christ accomplished this by breaking down the "middle wall of the partition." Some have supposed this terminology to have occurred to Paul because of the rending of the veil at the temple during the crucifixion. That, however, symbolized the removal of the barrier between sinners and God—not exactly the point here. Many today refer to the barricade separating the court of the Gentiles from the sanctuary proper in Jerusalem, which had placards affixed warning Gentiles of death if they tried to enter. The first century Jewish historian Josephus referred to it as "the middle wall." However, this barrier was not physically demolished until the destruction of the temple in A.D. 70 (nearly a decade after this letter), so that its destruction could hardly have suggested the analogy to Paul. The following verse seems to identify clearly the barrier as "the law of commandments" which was the great source of cleavage between Gentile and Jew.

This barrier is further described as enmity. In this context it refers not to the enmity between sinners and God, but between Jew and Gentile. This hostility was centered in the Mosaic law with its mandatory decrees which became the basis of a bitter exclusiveness to the Jew and a despised and ridiculed thing to Gentiles. Christ, however, by satisfying its demands and meeting its penalty, made the law inoperative. Thus the cause of estrangement between the two groups was removed.

Christ did more than simply ease the tension between Gentile and Jew. He created "one new man." Thus there are three orders of man in this passage: Gentile, Jew, and Christian. As a result of Christ's work in redemption and regeneration, those who formerly were categorized as either Gentile or Jew are made Christians by new birth. In this "new man," the former distinctions are irrelevant. Since Christ satisfied the Law and made it no longer operative, it is not now a question of forcing Gentiles to become proselytes and adopt Jewish practices. The Law with its distinctions was made inoperative for all believers, regardless of their ancestry. (Of course, the moral principles in the Mosaic law have always been God's will for men, and still are. It was wrong to murder, steal, or commit adultery long before the Ten Commandments appeared, and these things are still wrong. But as a law code, complete with sacrifices and penalties, it was fulfilled and abolished by Christ. See Heb 7:11-19.)

By thus dealing with the Mosaic law, and by imparting new life to believers, Christ ended the division between the two and succeeded in reconciling both to God in one body. (Explanations of the "one body" as Christ's physical body which was crucified are unlikely. The reference to the church by this metaphor is the same as 1 Co 10:17.) The enmity referred to in verse 16 is thought by some to refer to the hostility between men and God, and thus is a shift from its usage in verse 15. The fact that the two are inseparably interwoven makes the choice difficult, for the sacrifice of Christ which satisfied the Law made peace with God as well as wiping out the barrier between Jew and Gentile, and the former is basic to the latter. Nevertheless, the emphasis in the context is the relation of Jew and Gentile, and the use of "enmity" in verse 15 would argue for the same understanding of it in verse 16.

The announcement of this peace provided by Christ has been declared in the gospel. Christ is stated to be the one who preached it (2:17). This cannot refer to the incarnation, for peace was not achieved until His death, as the previous verses show. Nor can it refer to our Lord's postresurrection ministry, for this was confined to Jews. Rather, it refers to the proclamation of the gospel which Christ made through His Spirit-filled apostles. Such passages as Matthew 28:20, Luke 10:16, John 13:20, and Acts 10:26-38, convey this thought of Christ's identification with those who proclaim the gospel.

"You which were afar off" describes the Gentiles (cf. v. 13), and "them that were nigh" depicts Jews who possessed the Old Testament and the covenantal promises. Both groups had peace preached to them and have now become Christians. It should be noted that Paul refers to Gentiles in verse 17 as "you," but he does not speak of the Jews as "we." This is illustrative of the fact that he regards the present situation no longer as comprising two groups, with himself belonging to one of them, but as one body with former distinctions abolished.

In verse 18 all members of the Trinity are referred to. "Him" is clearly Christ the reconciler, and the Spirit and Father are explicitly mentioned. If the first word of the verse is translated "for" or "because," the verse becomes a confirmation of the previous statement by appealing to their experience. It is possible that it should be translated "that," and be regarded as introducing the content of this message of peace which Christ proclaimed. Either way the truth is affirmed that Christ has provided access for all believers to the Father. The word *access* includes the ideas of bringing and introducing. Not only has heaven's door been opened, but believers have been properly introduced to the Father. The Holy Spirit takes both groups (as individuals, of course) and implants regenerated life, so that they are now members of the same family—the family of God.

THE MAKING OF ONE BUILDING (2:19-22)

This concluding paragraph of the discussion moves from the metaphor of the church as one body to the picture of the church as one building, reinforcing the thought of the great unity of the church in which all true believers are on an equal footing.

The Gentile readers are no longer strangers as far as the promises of God are concerned. "Strangers" is a general term for those who are away from home, often descriptive of travelers or visitors. "Foreigners" describes noncitizens who may be living in the community but are not natives and have no rights as citizens. This was an apt description of Gentiles in relation to the salvation of God revealed in the Old Testament. But now they are "fellowcitizens with the saints." Because of Christ who made peace and broke down the partition,

Gentile believers are now fully-enfranchised citizens of God's heavenly kingdom, along with Jewish believers. "Saints" is used in the same sense as in 1:1, to describe Christian believers. Gentile converts are on an equal footing with Jewish Christians in the church. Both are saints and thus members of the household of God. The mention of a household connotes a warmer tone of family fellowship than the political metaphor of citizenship may have conveyed. It also provided an easy transition to the figure of a building, which is next developed.

In describing the church as a building, Paul states that believers are "built upon the foundation of the apostles and prophets." Because these apostles are undeniably the apostles of Christ, it seems most likely that the prophets here mentioned are New Testament prophets, not those from Old Testament times. The order of mention would suggest this (i.e., after apostles), as would the absence of the Greek article with "prophets," which shows them to belong to the same class as the apostles. Furthermore, the other two references to prophets in Ephesians are certainly to the New Testament order (3:5; 4:11).

A greater problem is involved in interpreting the expression "the foundation of the apostles." Is "apostles" appositional (i.e., the foundation which consists of the apostles)? Or does the term name the originating cause (i.e., the foundation which the apostles laid through their teaching)? Or is it a genitive of possession (i.e., the same foundation on which the apostles are built, viz., Christ)? All of these are true, and the choice is thus more difficult. Either of the first two seems more likely to this writer. To consider the apostles and prophets as the foundation harmonizes with Revelation 21:14, and would contain the thought that the office of apostle provided the New Testament scriptures. The fact that Christ is called the foundation by Paul in 1 Corinthians 3:11 does not prevent his using a different symbolism here. It should be noted that in the present figure, Christ is the cornerstone, a feature which may serve to distinguish Him from the foundation.

In this building Christ is the cornerstone. This is the significant stone in the building, which governs the lines and angles of all the others. So in the church it is Christ Himself who makes all believers "living stones" (1 Pe 2:4-5) and governs the place they hold in the building (Eph 4:7-8). And believers have become such by virtue of receiving the Word of God on the testimony of the apostles. Because of each believer's vital (i.e., life-sharing) union with Christ, he is part of this one building, the church. Each convert, whether he be Jew or Gentile, adds to the growth of the structure. And this structure is no less than a holy temple, for God dwells within it. If the Jewish temple at Jerusalem suggested Paul's figure, it is important to note that he chose the word that denoted the sanctuary proper, rather than one that described the outer courts and buildings. It was this inner sanctuary which was regarded as God's dwelling place.

The paragraph closes at verse 22 with the reminder that in this vital union ("in whom") with Christ "ye also" are a part of the building. Paul has never lost sight of his readers while discussing the grand theme of the church as Christ's body and as God's temple. Thus he mentions that the Ephesian Christians are personally involved. Each one is on an equal footing with every other Christian. Through regeneration all believers, whether Jew or Gentile, have been made recipients of eternal life, and have been made a part of that spiritual unity, the church. This true church is God's habitation in this world, for by His Holy Spirit He dwells in each believer individually and makes him a part of one spiritual organism, the church. Again we note all the members of the Trinity involved in the formation of the church: In Christ believers are formed into one body and one building, in connection with the work of the Spirit who regenerates and indwells, in order that we might form an habitation of God.

6

APOSTLE FOR THE GENTILES

PAUL'S STEWARDSHIP (3:1-4)

THIS SECTION BEGINS with a striking break in the grammatical structure—a device not infrequent with Paul, which captures attention by its very forcefulness. The subject "I Paul" has no verb, and probably none should be supplied at verse 1. The best sense is achieved by noting that the initial sentence is interrupted at verse 2. The original thought is then resumed at verse 14, as the repetition of "For this cause I" would suggest. It should not be thought, however, that verses 1-13 are merely parenthetical or of secondary importance (although they are a grammatical digression). The thought contained is highly relevant to the context.

"For this cause" refers to the thought of the previous section. It was because of God's grace in bringing together Gentile and Jew in the church and making them a habitation for Himself that Paul is thrilled in his soul (see 3:14). Even his present situation as a prisoner in Rome is viewed not as a personal catastrophe but related to divine purposes. He calls himself "the prisoner of Jesus Christ," meaning that even though he is presently confined, he belongs to Christ and it is in His service that this circumstance has occurred. In fact, Paul was in prison "for you Gentiles," because his preaching the gospel to Gentiles had been the cause of the troubles which eventually landed him in Rome (Ac 21—28).

"If" (3:2) may mean "if indeed" and indicate a supposition

which is taken for granted (in Gk, a first class condition, which is assumed to be true). It then is a polite way of saying, "I'm sure you have heard." It by no means implies that this letter was written to some place where Paul had never been. Arndt and Gingrich's *Greek-English Lexicon* gives the meaning "inasmuch as" for this expression,* and thus the statement asserts that Paul's position was well known.

Paul claims that the "dispensation of the grace of God" had been given to him. "Dispensation" is an old translation of a word that means administration, stewardship, or management. Here he refers to the phase of God's administration or program which had been particularly entrusted to him. This specific stewardship was his responsibility to proclaim the good news of God's grace to Gentiles, such as the Ephesians.

The particular stewardship with which Paul had been invested is said to be "the mystery" which came to him by revelation (3:3). It was not the product of his own study, nor was it imparted to him through any human instruction. It came by revelation from God. The term *mystery* is employed frequently in the New Testament, and appears six times in Ephesians. It refers not to something esoteric, but to that which was previously unknown and unknowable apart from divine revelation, and which has now been disclosed. The content of this particular mystery is defined in verse 6. It was the truth about the church, a new entity composed of Jews and Gentiles on an equal footing. Concerning this mystery Paul had written previously in brief. Although it is conceivable that he refers to some other letter now lost, it is more likely that he is referring to previous portions of this letter, particularly 2:11-22 and perhaps 1:22-23, in which the subject of the church as Christ's body, including Jews and Gentiles, had at least been touched upon. The verb tense would then be regarded as an epistolary aorist, and translated "I have written."

* William F. Arndt and F. Wilbur Gingrich, eds., *A Greek-English Lexicon of the New Testament*, p. 152.

A careful perusal of the foregoing passages will reveal the breadth of Paul's knowledge of this truth. He writes out of clear understanding of the doctrine, without any hint of doubt or speculation. "The mystery of Christ" (3:4) seems to be an enlargement of "the mystery" (v. 3). Christ is named as the object in whom all the truth about the church is contained and made possible. It is the mystery regarding Christ and His redeeming work which made possible the church.

PAUL'S MESSAGE (3:5-7)

Now in previous generations (i.e., in the O.T. period), this full revelation was not made known to mankind (3:5). To be sure, the idea of Gentile salvation was not a new one, even in the Old Testament, but what was not previously declared by God was that Gentiles might experience these blessings of salvation equally with Jews without themselves becoming Jews by proselytization. To the apostles and prophets of the New Testament era, however, this revelation was made. These are the same persons mentioned in 2:20. In the original text the use of one article ("the") with both nouns marks them as members of one class. In some cases, at least, they were the same persons, for apostles also prophesied. Paul was an apostle and a prophet. To call them "holy apostles" is not a mark of superstitious veneration from a later date, but an assertion that they were "set apart" by God as His instruments for this revelation. We note that Paul does not claim to be the only recipient of this revelation. Men like Peter (Ac 10) and Philip (Ac 8) received it also.

"By the Spirit" notes the fact that the Holy Spirit imparted the information. A good example is the case of Peter, who would not (by his own testimony) have gone to the Gentile Cornelius if the Spirit of God had not directly informed him that the barriers which once existed were now removed (Ac 10:1—11:18).

Paul conveys the substance of the mystery with three Greek

terms (3:6). The Gentiles are now revealed to be fellow-heirs, of the same body, and partakers of the promise. In the Greek text each of these nouns is compounded with the same prefix meaning "co-" or "fellow-." Thus he says that Gentiles are fellow-heirs, fellow-members, and fellow-partakers with Jews of these salvation blessings.

To call them fellow-heirs stresses the fact that believing Gentiles now have the same legal status as Jews so far as inheriting what God has promised is concerned. Two persons might be heirs of a rich man, one receiving a handsome legacy and the other a pittance. But in no sense is there a suggestion that the Gentiles' status as heirs is any less than that of believing Jews. By calling them fellow-members of the same body Paul calls attention to the equality of their vital relationship with God. Both groups are participants equally in the new life which comes in regeneration, just as all parts of a body are equally alive. As fellow-partakers of the promise in Christ Jesus, they are equal sharers of the blessings provided in salvation. The emphasis throughout this statement on the "fellow-" status of Gentiles with Jews can hardly be missed.

It is possible that Paul means by this "promise," the promise of the Holy Spirit which by its fulfilment in their lives made them members of the body of Christ. It was the reception of the Holy Spirit in regeneration by Gentiles which was the conclusive evidence to Peter and the Jewish segment of the church that God's purposes included the Gentiles in the church (Ac 15:8). Paul spoke of the blessing of Abraham which was now available to Gentiles through Christ, and equates this with their receiving "the promise of the Spirit through faith" (Gal 3:14). Probably, however, the promise is used in its widest sense to include all Christian blessings, among which are regeneration, membership in the body of Christ, and participation in the Messianic kingdom to come. All these blessings are the possession of the church through the gospel.

Paul rejoices in his privilege of ministering this gospel. He thinks back to his experience on the Damascus Road, when

Christ displayed His mighty power in arresting Paul's persecuting plans and transforming his life (3:7). The "gift" is defined as the "grace of God" (as made clear by v. 8). Paul regarded his ministry as the result of God's favor, unmerited in any way by Paul, but operating totally by God's effective energy which wrought such a dramatic change in the former persecutor.

PAUL'S COMMISSION (3:8-9)

As the apostle thinks of his commission from God, he does not want to convey the impression that he is exalting himself. He terms himself "less than the least" of all saints. The actual word employed is a superlative form with a comparative ending placed upon it. The translation in the King James Version conveys the sense well. Some students have felt that Paul may have been making a playful allusion to his own name, which literally meant "little." Certainly it was not false humility, but was occasioned by the remembrance of his persecuting record which God forgave in order to give his life this new direction. Similar self-deprecating statements of Paul are found in 1 Corinthians 15:8-9; 2 Corinthians 12:11; and 1 Timothy 1:15-16.

The "grace" which was given to Paul was not just salvation, but the particular ministry with which he was entrusted. This is made clear in verse 2 and following. It was his responsibility to proclaim the gospel to Gentiles. The latter part of verse 8 states the content of this grace, which constituted Paul's specific commission. His task was to take the message of salvation and declare it to Gentiles. This does not mean that he could not preach to Jews, for he often did this with the full blessing of God, but what was distinctive about his commission was its emphasis on Gentile evangelization. This message of salvation was the proclamation of Christ's unsearchable riches of grace for lost sinners. The wonder of it always thrilled the apostle, and he counted his commission a great privilege.

As a part of Paul's commission, it was his task to make it clear to all men what God's program was regarding the mystery of Gentile inclusion. To "make all men see" goes beyond mere proclamation, and involves actual enlightenment. In the day in which Paul wrote, these things were not clearly recognized. Even Christians (particularly Jewish ones) often failed to understand the basis of Gentile inclusion in the church. To Paul was given the task to make it clear. "Fellowship" (KJV, 3:9) should be replaced by some word such as *administration* or *management*. Paul was commissioned to clarify how God was administering affairs regarding salvation particularly as Gentiles were involved. This was a mystery in the sense explained in verse 3. It was now a revealed truth, but formerly it had not been disclosed. From ages past the plan to form one new body of believers in Christ had been hidden. It was no afterthought, however, for all the time it was hidden in God, that is, in His mind and purpose. But only now in connection with the apostles' ministry was it made known to the world. God is referred to in His capacity as creator of all things. It reminds us that in view of God's creatorship of all things, even the church was in God's plan at the beginning, and thus this new development is in perfect harmony with all creation.

GOD'S PURPOSE (3:10-11)

God's exalted plan for the church involves the greatest of extremes. He chose a most unlikely man as His apostle (3:8) and intended to use him and the church to reveal truth to angels (v. 10)! "Principalities and powers in heavenly places" refers not to human authorities but to ranks of angels, as in numerous other passages (1:21; 6:12; Ro 8:38; Col 1:16; 1 Pe 3:22). That angels have an interest in the redemption of mankind is expressed in 1 Peter 1:12. They are also ministering spirits to the church (Heb 1:14). Paul has previously stated that the mystery of Gentile inclusion had been hidden from the ages past. <u>Thus angels, who had witnessed the fall of man, never knew until the revelation of the mystery of the church how God would achieve this grand unity through the church.</u> They had known how God had chosen Israel and given His word and promises to that nation. Gentiles, however, seemed to be excluded unless they became proselytes, and this was comparatively seldom.

Through the church, however, after centuries of bitterness, cross purposes, and almost total division, Jew and Gentile are united on equal terms by faith in Christ and become one new body (2:16). Angels, who serve God continually and carry out His orders, are thus made aware of the infinite scope and wisdom of His plan which provided redemption for lost humanity.

The redemption of both Jew and Gentile and their inclusion in the church was in accord with God's eternal purpose. This purpose was formed in connection with Christ. Even though the plan was hidden in past ages, it was fully prepared and merely waited its proper season for fulfillment. Now that Christ has come and accomplished it by His atoning death, the plan has become a fact for all to see—even the angels in heaven.

ENCOURAGEMENT FOR THE EPHESIANS (3:12-13)

After speaking of the sublime purpose of the church in which God displays His wisdom to such an extent that even angels are impressed, a lowly Christian might be overcome with awe and shrink from a full use of his privileges. Paul, therefore, hastens to reassure every believer of what this means to him personally. By using the terms *boldness, access,* and *confidence,* he stresses the fact of the believer's status with God through Christ. "Boldness" sometimes refers to freedom of speech or prayer, but here it has the larger sense of freedom of spirit (cf. Phil 1:20; 1 Ti 3:13). "Access" and "confidence" denote that ready entrance without hesitation which is the prerogative of those who have proper authorization. The believer's authority is not any merit of his own, but is dependent solely on the merits of his Saviour, Jesus Christ. It is by our faith in Him ("Him" is an objective genitive in the Gk text) that this access is freely ours. Thus it is in the church, which is Christ's body (1:22-23), in which prefect communion is established between believers and God.

In view of God's great accomplishment in bringing Gentiles and Jews together in the church, Paul urges the Ephesians not to grow discouraged in their Christian lives. Particularly, he has in view the possibility that his long imprisonment might cause some Christians to become disheartened. (Grammatically, it is possible for the clause to be understood as "I ask that I faint not in my tribulations." However, Paul's consistent rejoicing in trials causes this explanation to be rejected by most interpreters.) Paul's imprisonment must have stretched into about five years by this time (two years in Caesarea, voyage to Rome and winter spent on Malta, plus up to two years in Rome). Some of his readers may have wondered whether the program of evangelizing was worthwhile in view of the risks involved. They may also have wondered whether the work was going to stop, inasmuch as the apostle was prevented from his normal duties.

It was true that his present sufferings had been incurred through his efforts to win Gentiles. This was the cause of the violent Jewish hatred he experienced (as well as some hostility even from Jewish Christians). But rather than regard this as an occasion for gloom, Paul says they should understand what was transpiring as their "glory." They should feel honored that in God's plan their salvation was important enough for His apostle to undergo such rigors. Of course, they would not be glad that Paul was suffering, but they could rejoice in its purpose and what it was accomplishing. If God permitted such suffering in His apostle, how highly He must value the church for whose advancement these sufferings had been incurred.

7

PAUL'S SECOND PRAYER FOR HIS READERS

3:14-21

THE FIRST PRAYER in this epistle was expressed in 1:15-23. The emphasis was on spiritual knowledge which Paul desired each believer to possess. In the second prayer, the emphasis is on love, based on the love of Christ, and exercised in spiritual growth.

THE ONE ADDRESSED (3:14-15)

"For this cause" repeats the very words of 3:1, showing that Paul actually had this prayer in view at that point, but had paused to give further elaboration to the great truths he had been setting forth regarding the union of Gentile and Jew in the church. Since 3:2-13 is a discussion of the same truth as set forth in the verses just preceding 3:1, it is rightly understood that "for this cause" in both 3:1 and 3:14 refers to these same truths.

The bodily posture of bowing the knees is a common one in Scripture, although not the only one (see 1 Ki 8:54; Lk 22:41; Ac 7:60; 9:40; 20:36; 21:5). It is a posture which reflects the attitude of heart in acknowledging the greatness of God, and is especially appropriate at this point. The wonder of God's plan as seen in the church should drive any Christian to his knees.

God the Father is here addressed as the one of whom the whole family in heaven and earth is named. Absence of the

Greek article causes many to insist on the translation "every family." However, a similar use without the article occurs at 2:21 ("whole building"), and numerous other instances of omission of the article before "all" with singular nouns (such as "all power," Mt 28:18; "all the house of Israel," Ac 2:36) show this to be an acceptable idiom. This usage fits very well with the context where Paul has been discussing the new oneness of Gentiles and Jews in Christ.

<u>In referring to the whole family of God, Paul is not speaking of a universal fatherhood of God,</u> but of those who have a spiritual kinship to God as their Father. See 2:18-19 especially, as well as the whole passage 2:11—3:13. He is speaking <u>soteriologically, not universally.</u> This spiritual family of God includes all who truly acknowledge God as their heavenly Father, whether they be Jewish or Gentile saints on earth, Old Testament saints now in heaven, or saints of coming ages. The expression may possibly include also the holy angels, cherubim, seraphim, and other spirit beings.

THE REQUESTS DESIRED (3:16-19)

The first request is that the Ephesians might be granted spiritual strengthening so that Christ would dwell in them (3:16-17). Such a gift can be measured only by the wealth embodied in God's own glory. The resources of such a giver are beyond human estimation. Of course, it would take this sort of giver to provide what Paul asks. He desires that his readers be strengthened by God's power through the agency of the Holy Spirit. The Spirit comes to reside in each believer at regeneration, but must be relied upon continually to furnish power for Christian living.

The divine strengthening here desired will be experienced "in the inner man." "In" is actually the word *into,* and may suggest the penetration of spiritual power into the very core of the believer's being. It is not the outward, visible, physical person that is in view here, but the immaterial part of man which controls him. God's Spirit operates within the believer, prompting his mind and spirit to respond more perfectly to God's will and thus to exhibit more and more Christlikeness (cf. Col 3:10).

Some regard verse 17 as the second petition in this prayer, parallel to verse 16. However, it seems better to recognize it as the result intended from the strengthening desired in verse 16. Spiritual strengthening was not sought for its own sake, but in order that Christ might dwell in them. Inasmuch as these words clearly refer to the Ephesian Christians, Paul cannot be referring to the initial indwelling of believers by Christ in the person of the Holy Spirit. Rather, he is speaking of the further and richer dwelling which occurs as Christ takes possession of more and more of us. This is expressed elsewhere as "filling." As the Spirit of God indwells believers (also called the Spirit of Christ, Ro 8:9), He provides spiritual strength as we by faith appropriate the truth of God's Word and present our lives to His control. This commitment of life to Christ's control brings about His fuller occupancy of our lives. All of this is possible when believers have been rooted and grounded in love. When they are securely settled in the love of God, recognizing what this love has meant, they are moved to return this love through an ever growing commitment to Christ (1 Jn 4:19).

The second petition of this prayer is that the Ephesians may more fully understand the love of Christ (3:18-19). Although many understand the previous participles ("rooted and grounded") as belonging to the thought of verse 18, in the original sentence structure, the conjunction "in order that" follows them, and thus seems to leave them with the foregoing material. The two chief petitions of this prayer are very closely connected in thought, however, so that the reference of these terms is not vitally important.

Paul asks of God that his readers "may be able to comprehend." Literally, it is "be made strong to comprehend." The thought expressed is more detailed than simply "that ye may comprehend" would have been. It calls attention to the fact that before spiritual comprehension can occur, there must be a spiritual strengthening of the believer by the power of God. This parallels very closely the thought of verse 16, where strengthening occurs by God's power. "With all saints" reminds the Ephesians that Paul is not speaking of some special spiritual information available only to a few, but is praying for that which all Christians may share.

He wants them to understand "what is the breadth, and length, and depth, and height." Because Paul does not specify breadth of "what," all sorts of objects have been suggested. The church, redemption, the mystery, the wisdom of God—all have been proposed, as well as others. Some have seen in this four-dimensional reference a description of the cross or the temple. The very absence of any expressed object, however, would lead us to conclude that he was not thinking in any of the above categories. It seems, rather, that the object in view is explained in the next verse as the divine love which is immeasurable, and yet which is basic to our Christian experience. As Christians we have had our roots placed in the love which God displayed for us in sending his Son (3:17). Now Paul desires that we all have an increase of spiritual discernment to appreciate just what God has done.

This is further elaborated in verse 19, where the "and" does not name an additional request but an elaboration of what has just been said, or at least showing a close relationship to it. All Christians need to increase their comprehension of the love of Christ, here said to be surpassing knowledge. Paul is not asking for the unattainable. But even though a complete knowledge of Christ's love, which brought redemption, made possible the church, and secured the blessings of the Christian life for now and eternity, may remain beyond our capacity, there is a real comprehension possible for us.

The result contemplated from this greater perception of the love of Christ is the filling of believers in reference to all the fullness of God. God's fullness is that with which He is filled, and denotes the perfections and excellencies He possesses.

"With all the fulness" is not the best translation, for no believer could possibly contain all the fullness of God. A better rendering of the phrase is "with respect to all the fullness of God." He is the unlimited source from which we draw for all the spiritual resources we need.

THE GLORY ASCRIBED (3:20-21)

This doxology draws the prayer to its close. Paul finds in God the one to whom he can pray in faith because He is abundantly able to accomplish the things asked for. He uses a word which expresses the highest form of comparison imaginable. The term, compounded from three words, conveys the idea of superabundance and more besides.

God is able, says Paul, to respond to the believer's prayers in ways that go far beyond what we might dare to ask for or even what we might contemplate. <u>We cannot ask beyond God's ability to fulfil.</u> So often our asking fails to understand what blessed spiritual joys God wants to provide us. We are too frequently content with the supply of temporal and physical needs. So much of our asking is selfish in nature and without awareness of the higher goals God has for us. Paul reminds us by these words that even the tremendous requests which he has just voiced to God are by no means wishful thinking or beyond the possibility of any real fulfillment (3:16-19).

On the contrary, these requests will be answered by the same divine power which already is operating within each believer. Inasmuch as God is indwelling every believer, and thus each child of God already is experiencing the power of God working in his life, this doxology should remind us that answers to our prayers are strongly assured. What encouragement it is to realize that the believer's growth in comprehending the love of Christ and his increasing experience of Christ's occupancy of his life are accomplished by God's own power operating in him. He has made every provision for man's salvation, both in its initiation at regeneration and in its continuation through the Christian life.

Consequently, all the glory belongs to God. The older manuscripts say, "To Him be the glory in the church and in Christ Jesus unto all the generations forever and ever." "In the church" should probably be understood in the same way as "in Christ Jesus." The thought is that glory belongs to God because of what He has accomplished in the church, and this was all made possible in connection with Christ. Because of the vital union with Christ in the church, Gentiles and Jews are now one in the family of God. Thus Paul wishes God to be glorified in connection with the church which demonstrates His saving grace, and in connection with Christ Jesus, whose redemptive work made it possible.

Part Three

DUTIES OF THE CHURCH

4:1—6:20

8

WALK IN UNITY

4:1-16

THIS SECOND MAJOR DIVISION of the letter emphasizes the responsibilities of believers as a consequence of the doctrinal truths elaborated in the earlier chapters. Paul follows his characteristic pattern of presenting the doctrinal foundation and then drawing on this basis for practical exhortations.

THE COMMAND (4:1-3)

"Therefore" is a logical connective, causing the reader to regard what follows as a reasonable deduction from what has just been said. By designating himself as "the prisoner in the Lord," Paul is not making a plea for sympathy, but rather is testifying to his acceptance of present circumstances as God's will. Although his movements among the churches are restricted, he nevertheless has no doubt that he is "in the Lord" (so reads the Gk text). He may also be understood as explaining that his being a prisoner was in relation to the Lord. He was under detention for no other reason.

The command is that believers walk in a manner worthy of the calling by which God had called them. The term *vocation* as found in the King James Version must not be understood in the modern specialized sense of "occupation." Nor is Paul talking about certain Christians who are engaged in specialized ministries. Paul's word meant "calling," and that calling of God which each believer has received and which constitutes believers as saints (Ro 1:6-7). This calling of believers has been described in chapters 1—3. Now appropriate conduct should follow. No believer is worthy in himself to merit the salvation which he enjoys, but he is expected to live in such a manner as befits the purposes God has planned for him. "Walk" is an excellent metaphor to describe the Christian life, for it pictures the daily activity and progress of life.

This worthy walk of the Christian must involve the display of lowliness or humility. Here is an attitude of mind which demands a true estimate of oneself as he is in God's sight. Interestingly, this characteristic was not much admired in the Greco-Roman world in which these early Christians moved. To them it seemed to mean a groveling spirit, unworthy of the ideal man. The Bible, however, in both Old and New Testaments emphasizes the truth that God does not look upon these characteristics through the same eyes as fallen man. He resists the proud and gives grace to the lowly (Pr 3:34; 1 Pe 5:5). Closely allied with lowliness is meekness, which stresses gentleness as one way of displaying a humble attitude of mind.

Long-suffering is that quality which endures vexations for a considerable period of time without retaliation. It commonly describes one's relations toward other people, and this sense is appropriate here where unity among believers is the theme. Long-suffering is further explained as "forbearing one another in love." The action described is of putting up with the other person, not with any spirit of bitterness or of resignation, but in true Christian love.

The command is summarized in verse 3 by urging the Ephesians to give diligence continually to keep the unity of the Spirit. We note that Paul does not imply we are to create this unity, but are to maintain what already exists. The statement also suggests that the accomplishment of this command will not be automatic or always easy. We must give diligence continually (lit. meaning of "endeavouring," KJV) to preserve this oneness. The bond of peace is that unifying atmosphere in which God, the author of peace, accomplishes His will in the church. Paul does not call for merely an outward show of unanimity in which some may be writhing inwardly with discontent, but for that true peace of heart which accompanies spiritual unity.

THE BASIS (4:4-6)

The following paragraph in the epistle emphasizes the sevenfold oneness that believers share, and this provides the great incentive to maintain a Christian walk in true unity.

Verse 4 names the first three items, and there is special mention of the Holy Spirit, the third Person of the Trinity. There is "one body" in which all believers are incorporated. Paul refers to the church, as is clear from such passages as Romans 12:5: "So we, being many, are one body in Christ, and every one members one of another." The fact that this is a present spiritual reality is the basis for Christian living that avoids divisiveness. A body is not just a collection of parts but a coordinated and living organism. In just this way the church should manifest its oneness.

"One Spirit" refers to the Holy Spirit, who has been God's agent in placing believers into Christ and thus constituting them as one body (1 Co 12:13). The Spirit is also the one who indwells each believer and imparts divine life so that all believers collectively form a living spiritual body. It is similar to the circumstance of the various parts of the human body constituted as one being by the presence of the soul.

Believers also possess one hope, by virtue of their calling from God. This common goal they share refers to the glorious future when Christ's coming will bring to its consummation the great work of redemption.

The second triad, found in verse 5, emphasizes the Son of God. The "one Lord" to whom all believers give allegiance is the Lord Jesus Christ. The "one faith" may be regarded either objectively, as the body of truth ("the faith which was once delivered unto the saints," Jude 3) without which one cannot be a Christian and thus would have no basis for unity; or subjectively, as the believer's trust which has been placed in Christ. Perhaps it is unnecessary to draw too sharp a distinction, for one's subjective faith must have the truth as its object.

"One baptism" is usually explained as water baptism, the initiatory rite by which the convert gives testimony to his faith. However, it could also refer to Spirit baptism, whereby the believer is made a part of the body of Christ. An interesting parallel is found in 1 Corinthians 12:12-13, in which four expressions of Ephesians 4:4-6 ("one body," "one Spirit," "one Lord," "one baptism") appear as "one body," "one Spirit," "Christ," and "baptized." In the 1 Corinthians parallel, the baptism referred to is clearly Spirit baptism, and this would support such an identification in Ephesians 4:5.

The capstone in this list of seven is the one God and Father. The fatherhood stated here refers to God's relation to all believers. The three prepositions designate God as sovereign and transcendent ("above all"), as operating "through" His children in accomplishing His will, and as residing "in" them.

THE DIVINE GIFTS (4:7-13)

Paul first issues a statement that God has bestowed gifts to believers to enable them to accomplish the goal of walking in unity (4:7). The previous paragraph has emphasized the fact of unity by pointing to the oneness of believers in various respects. Now Paul shows that each believer is an individual participant and recipient of the divine graces which he needs. "Grace" (charis, 4:7) is apparently the equivalent of charisma, the more common New Testament term for the various spiritual gifts bestowed by Christ upon believers. It could, however, refer to the inward subjective grace from God which then results in charisma, the gift as manifested (so Expositor's Greek Testament).*

Each person's "grace" is in proportion to what Christ in His

* S. D. F. Salmond, "The Epistle to the Ephesians," in The Expostior's Greek Testament, 3:323.

sovereign wisdom has freely given. Not all receive the same gifts, or the same number of gifts, or the same amount of any one gift. Christ dispenses as He deems best.

The scriptural proof (4:8-10) cited for the above assertion is drawn from Psalm 68:18. "When he ascended up on high, he led captivity captive, and gave gifts unto men." The historical circumstances of the psalm are uncertain. It depicts a victorious and triumphant return, probably of David to Mount Zion. If the psalm was intended to be Messianic (as this usage in Ephesians certainly suggests), then David is regarded as typical of his greater son whose passion victory was followed by the ascension.

The chief points in the quotation which were significant to the author were the victorious ascent and the dispensing of gifts to men. Certain other features, however, are also of special interest. "He led captivity captive" is translated "he captured prisoners" (Jer. Bible), "he took many captives with him" (TEV), and "he led a host of captives" (RSV). Messianically interpreted, this is usually referred to Christ's conquering of His enemies: Satan, sin, death, the curse. Others (a minority, but including many of the ancient Fathers) explain these "captives" as friends, either the redeemed on earth, or Old Testament saints in hades (Heb., *sheol*). In support of this last interpretation, arguments such as the following are given:

1. That which is led captive is taken to heaven. This is not true of Satan, sin, death, or the curse.

2. The past tense (aorist) "led captive" does not fit the regeneration of subsequent believers as well as some prior action.

3. The interpretation that this refers to the descent of Christ to the realm of the dead at His death accords well with 1 Peter 3:19-20.

4. It fits Matthew 27:50-53, where the visible release of some Old Testament saints from hades may imply the spiritual release of all such.

5. This harmonizes with the apparent change in location of

paradise, which in the New Testament era is stated as being above, and equated with heaven (2 Co 12:2-4).

Paul has made a slight change in the quotation by translating "gave" instead of the Hebrew (and LXX) term in Psalm 68:18 which meant "received." However, the Hebrew word was often used proleptically in the sense of "taking" from someone in order to give to others (e.g., Gen 34:4, "he took a wife for his son" means "he gave his son a wife"). Thus the conqueror characteristically celebrated his victory by dispensing from his bounty (which in the historical setting of the psalm had been obtained through spoil).

Verses 9 and 10 apply the quotation to Christ. The fact that an ascent was stated implies a prior descent. Inasmuch as the author attributes the passage to Christ, the ascent refers to Christ's ascension to heaven. Thus the previous descent must refer to the first coming of the Son of God to earth.

The phrase, "the lower parts of the earth," offers problems to the interpreter. Most modern interpreters explain "of the earth" as appositional, and explain the passage as referring to the incarnation in which Christ came from heaven to earth, and then later ascended from earth to heaven. By this interpretation, "lower parts" may refer to the lowly, humiliating aspects of His earthly career.

Earlier writers (and some recent ones) treat "of the earth" as a partitive or comparative genitive, and relate the statement to Christ's descent to hades (1 Pe 3:19-20). If this be correct, then Paul is showing the great extent of this descent, even to the realm where souls of the dead were held captive. Hence the ascent which followed is all the more impressive.

The very one who made such a remarkable descent is the same one who has now ascended. The Son of God left His home and position in heaven to identify Himself with humanity in order to save them. In so doing, He shared their humanity even including death. Now this has been followed by victory. Christ's ascension has taken Him to the most exalted height. Thus He is in a position to accomplish the divine purpose for the universe whereby all things are brought into proper order in Him. Christ, in whom dwells all the fullness of the Godhead (Col 2:9), is now, since His exaltation, able to fill all things with His presence. This includes the earth and the realm of the dead as well as His exalted position in heaven.

The *nature and purpose* of these gifts is explained in verses 11-13. Verse 7 suggested the bestowal of Christ's grace on believers individually. Verse 11 describes certain gifts given by Christ to the church as a whole, which of course are for the benefit of all believers.

Apostles (as well as the other gifts mentioned here) is a predicate accusative. A good translation of the phrase would be, "He gave some as apostles" or "He gave some to be apostles." The point is not that He gave to some men the gift of apostleship, but that the church as a whole received apostles as a gift from Christ. These men should probably be understood in the restricted sense as the Twelve plus Paul. Apostles were the authoritative founders of the church (2:20). The text does not say that the gift of apostles would be possessed by the church at all times. However, the results of this gift continue today in the New Testament which they gave us.

Prophets were persons who received direct revelation from God in the beginning days of the church before the New Testament revelation was written. The term seems to be used here in this restricted sense, rather than with the wider meaning of any who proclaimed the revelation received by others. Agabus is one example of a New Testament prophet (Ac 11:27-28; 21:10-11); so also are the five men in Acts 13:1, and the four daughters of Philip (Ac 21:9). This gift, along with the preceding one, seems to have ceased with the apostolic age, being superseded by the full revelation in the New Testament scripture.

The last gifts in the list appear to be permanent, with manifestations in the church today. *Evangelists* are itinerant preachers who have no permanent flock to care for. These have a modern counterpart in the present-day missionary as well as the more formally styled "evangelist." *Pastors and teachers* are named as one grammatical unit (by use of just one article in the Gk text). Inasmuch as the teaching of God's truth is basic to all pastoral care, the two items form a natural combination. It should be noted that in the New Testament both of these functions are exercised by the elder (i.e., bishop): "Elders . . . feed the flock" (1 Pe 5:1-2); "A bishop . . . must be . . . apt to teach" (1 Ti 3:2). The pastor-teacher describes the person whose responsibilities are usually localized, in contrast to the evangelist.

The three phrases of verse 12 have been treated as coordinates by the King James Version, as though these gifts were given to accomplish three equal ends. However, the threefold use of the English preposition "for" is not the best reflection of the underlying Greek text, where the first preposition differs from the last two. Thus it is preferable to regard the phrases either as successive, or the last two as elaborations of the first.

To regard them as successive offers the clearest progression of thought. The exercise of these Christ-given gifts was intended to coordinate and equip all believers for the work of ministry. ("Ministry" is used here in the general sense of service, not in the more restricted sense of official function.) Every believer, regardless of background, ability, or status, has a service to perform in the cause of Christ on earth. The gifts of apostle and prophet (i.e., for us, the N.T.), evangelist, and pastor-teacher provided the instruction, admonition, and spiritual nurture that are needed to achieve concerted action out of a diversity of individual Christians.

This ministering by all believers, as they have been equipped by the gifts just mentioned, is intended to accomplish the building up of the church. Although the idea of numerical growth may be involved, the emphasis in the passage seems to be on spiritual life and its development. We should observe that Scripture lays this responsibility on "the saints," that is, _all_ believers, not just the pastor or certain officials of the church. Every believer is expected by Christ to perform a ministry that will strengthen the church. The leaders, who have been given to the church by Christ as His gift, are to equip them so that the work can be accomplished.

The gifts just enumerated and the procedures outlined have as their purpose the arrival of all believers at a state of unity of the faith. There is a unity of faith already possessed by true believers (4:5), but there is also an experiential development of this faith as believers increase in spiritual capacity. This is closely connected with the Christian's growth in knowledge of the Son of God. The more that believers know of Him, the better able they are to trust Him.

Such development in the Christian life has as its aim the acquiring of spiritual maturity. The "perfect man" (4:13) referred to means a mature, full-grown man, in contrast to an infant (see next v.). Absolute perfection is not achieved in this life. Yet there is a relative maturity which is not only attainable but which is expected of every believer. Here the phrase is further explained by the next words, "the measure of the stature of the fulness of Christ." The church itself is called the fullness of Christ in 1:23. In 4:13 Paul speaks of that Christlikeness which each believer should display. That full spiritual development displayed by our Lord while on earth He desires to reproduce in us. The final achievement must await His coming, when "we shall be like him" (1 Jn 3:2), but now there is a "measure" of this Christlikeness which we should experience and demonstrate.

THE GOAL (4:14-16)

The ultimate goal toward which the injunction to walk in unity was directed is stated to be the production of maturity in each believer's life so that the whole church as Christ's body may function as a true organism with genuine coordination and growth.

Certain dangers, however, must be avoided. Believers who are spiritually immature are as helpless as infants. They are likened to persons with no knowledge of seamanship adrift on a stormy sea. The great danger to immature faith is false doctrine; it is here compared to strong winds which toss about an unguided boat. Such false doctrine is always being promoted by crafty men who by trickery and scheming lead their victims into spiritual disaster. Paul and the other apostles continually confronted such attacks in the early church. Colossians 2 describes one such instance in which human philosophy was promoted in the church at the expense of God's truth. The warning has always been pertinent, and is no less so today.

In contrast to the dangerous actions just described, believers are to strive for the goal of full spiritual maturity in Christ. This involves being truthful in all of our speech and dealings. The translation "speaking the truth" represents a Greek participle that may have a wider scope than just speech. If English would allow it, some such translation as "truthing it" would come closer to conveying the sense. The chief danger to spiritual babies (4:14) is the falsity and deceit employed by those who would entice them toward either heretical doctrine or unworthy conduct. Absolute truthfulness should characterize the speech and conduct of the one who shares the life of Christ. All truth, however, should be expressed "in love." Orthodoxy has not always been noted for this virtue. Paul is not saying that truth may on occasion be sacrificed in the interests of love, but he does insist that it must always be maintained in a spirit of love.

Spiritual growth can occur in such an atmosphere. Human bodies normally grow with all parts in proper relation to each other. The church, which is the body of Christ, must grow in relation to its head. As individual members of His body, we are to grow "into Him," or in relation to Him as the object of our faith and as the norm and controller of our spiritual development. "In all things" refers to all those elements of faith and character which should reach spiritual maturity.

Verse 16 explains that Christ the head is not only the object and standard of our spiritual growth ("into him," 4:15), but that <u>He is also the source of our growth</u>. He is the one "out of whom" the whole body receives its life and its coordination. This verse is similar to Colossians 2:19. As the human body receives its vitality and direction in all its parts through the joints which hold it together, unite it to its head, and make possible communication, nourishment, and coordinated action, so the church is supplied by its head with all that it requires for spiritual growth.

Now, the proper functioning of all interrelated parts is necessary for normal growth in a human body. Any overactivity of one part may result in a misshapen, monstrous organism. In the same way each member of Christ's body (i.e., individual Christians) is to exercise his ministry (4:11) and thus contribute to the upbuilding of the whole church. If even one Christian fails to develop spiritually, the church as a whole is not as strong as it ought to be. By growing spiritually as we ought, the unity of the body of Christ is preserved, the witness of the church in the world is maintained, and the growth of the church as a whole is accomplished.

9

AVOID PAGAN CONDUCT

4:17—5:21

THE OLD LIFE DESCRIBED (4:17-19)

As PAUL BEGINS this section of admonition regarding specific items of conduct, he solemnly asserts that these injunctions are "in the Lord." That is, Christ Himself is the authority behind them, and the apostle issues them with the full consciousness that he is no mere moralizer, but is testifying in his capacity as the Lord's spokesman.

The readers are urged to walk no longer as the Gentiles. The church at Ephesus had both Jews and Gentiles in it, but it was surrounded by a Gentile population. Thus to say that they should not walk as Gentiles was to say that their lives should not be conformed to the standards of the pagan world around them, but should be characterized by the new life they had received from Christ. The original text did not contain the word *other* (4:17). It is at least to be suggested that the writer is therefore not regarding his readers primarily as Gentiles (although they were), but as a distinct group. As Christians they are no longer merely to be categorized as Jews or Gentiles, but as members of a new body with distinctive features.

What is characteristic of individuals apart from God is the "vanity of their mind." "Vanity" here does not refer to pride, but to purposelessness, aimlessness, uselessness. "Mind" involves more than just intellect in this passage, for volition and aim are included. The mind of the unconverted man may be filled with many things, and may be highly developed in its intellectual attainments, but spiritually it is wholly unable to apprehend the life of God. Those who are apart from God are in a state of darkness in their spiritual understanding. Even though the evidence of God lies all about them in creation, as well as by direct revelation in Scripture, their understanding is darkened so that it cannot perceive the light which is available to them. Therefore, they are alienated from the life of God. This does not mean merely that they do not lead godly lives, but that they are separated from the divine life which God imparts to believers through Christ (Jn 14:6; 1 Jn 5:12).

This ignorance of God is stated as "in them." The form of expression suggests that Paul means more than just a casual statement that unbelievers are ignorant of God. A literal rendering would be, "the ignorance, the one being in them." It emphasizes this ignorance as basic and ingrained. Yet men cannot escape responsibility for this condition (cf. Ro 1:21-28). Thus Paul indicates here that it is due to the "hardness [not "blindness," KJV] of their heart." By rejecting that general revelation of God which may be clearly seen (Ro 1:20-21), they became insensitive and hardened. The figure suggests a callus which makes man's normal being unresponsive to God, in spite of his boasted intellect and other accomplishments.

"Being past feeling" (4:19) occurs only this once in the New Testament. It describes the pagan situation morally in a fashion consistent with their "hardness" of heart asserted in 4:18. Unbelievers were (and still are) generally insensitive to things moral and spiritual. They are spiritually calloused, failing to discern the sort of conduct that is morally right, or the features in their own behavior that are spiritually reprehensible.

This being so, they gave "themselves over to lasciviousness." The noun depicts debauchery, outrageous sensuality, wantonness. Their mode of life was neither an accidental nor a reluctant falling into error, but an act of choice. In Romans 1:24, 26, 28, Paul states that God gave them up. The apostle did not contradict himself. He has merely named both the human and the divine side of the situation. F. F. Bruce states it this way: "But one of the ways in which the wrath of God works is by giving sinners up to the course of their own choosing, with its terrible consequences."* *Expositor's Greek Testament* explains, "It is at once a guilty choice of men and a judicial act of God."†

Having abandoned themselves to this way of life, men without God have removed all hindrances to the practicing of moral uncleanness. This need not be limited to sexual sins, although certainly these are capable of great variety. "All" uncleanness suggests the widest possible scope. The ancient world with its sacred prostitutes and festal orgies gives abundant testimony to the attitudes of the day regarding sexual excesses, and these pagan customs were by no means unknown at Ephesus (whose temple with its many-breasted goddess was known far and wide). Nor is this description out of date for present-day society. Recent trends in the theater, television, styles of dress, and codes of behavior testify to the same condition of human hearts apart from the purifying work of God.

"With greediness" is not added as a separate and coordinate sin (that is, covetousness), but describes the manner in which these sins of uncleanness were indulged. They were practiced greedily, no one sin serving to satiate the sinner but merely making him desire more.

THE NEW LIFE COMMANDED (4:20-24)

The pagan life just sketched may have characterized these Ephesian Christians in the past, but a change had occurred. "Ye" is emphatic in the sentence. The sense is, "As for you, you did not in this manner learn Christ." Paul refers to their acceptance of the preaching of Christ regarding His person and work. By responding to Him and becoming Christians, they

* F. F. Bruce, *The Epistle to the Ephsians,* p. 92.
† S. D. F. Salmond, "The Epistle to the Ephesians," in *The Expositor's Greek Testament,* ed. W. R. Nicoll, 3:340.

had been born again, receiving the very life of God. This
obligated them to live in a manner appropriate to the Christ
whose name they bore and whose life they shared. It should
have been quite clear that the Christ whom they had received
expected from them a vastly different sort of life. Pagans responded to their gods by all kinds of excesses; Christians were
to respond to their God with conduct consistent with discipleship with Christ.

The conditional clause "if so be" does not imply doubtful-
ness as to its fulfillment, but uses the form which Greek
grammarians call a first class condition. It assumes that the
condition is true. The statement could be paraphrased, "You
did hear, didn't you?" By employing such a device, each reader
was forced to consider the question and answer it for himself,
and to answer it affirmatively (as the writer fully expects) was
to place oneself under obligation to its implications.

These readers were residents of Ephesus, and had surely
never heard Christ's physical voice. Hence this hearing must
refer to the hearing of Christ's voice in their hearts by the
Spirit at conversion. "And in Him ye were taught" is a more
literal translation ("in him" is not agency here, as KJV suggests). Paul means that as believers they were now in vital
union with Christ, and in that sphere their spiritual instruction
had proceeded.

"As the truth is in Jesus" emphasizes the fact that spiritual
truth which brought the great transformation to their former
lives was embodied in Jesus. It was not to be found in the
ungodly creeds and conduct of the old life. Thus this phrase
repeats the thought of verse 20, in which Paul states that his
readers had "learned Christ."

The content of the Christian instruction which they had
received is expressed by the three infinitives in 4:22-24 ("to
put off," "to be renewed," "to put on"). Two of them use
the imagery of the wardrobe ("put off," "put on"). Believers
had been taught in connection with their Christian commitment
to put off from themselves "the old man." This refers to the

natural self, which is dominated by sin. The similar passage
in Colossians 3:9-10 states that believers have already put off
the old man and have put on the new man. Ephesians 4:22
seems to command them to do so. Apparently Paul, who wrote
both passages, was looking at the same truth from two aspects.
At conversion, all believers become new creatures in Christ
(2 Co 5:17), and thus put on the "new man." Yet there is
always a need for spiritual realities to be translated into daily
living. Even though at regeneration the "old man" was dealt
a mortal blow and removed from unchallenged dominance in
the life, he is not yet dead. Each believer must reckon the old
life as dead and present himself to the control of the Spirit
(Col 3:5; Ro 6:11-13). The old life, as described in 4:18-19,
is ever trying to entice believers, but they must be done with
it, for it is in the process of corruption. The deceitful power
of sin dominates the old man, and it can only bring defeat
through the sinful desires which it stimulates. It is one's Christian duty to "put off" the old man in practice as well as in
creed.

The second infinitive in this series of three which convey
the content of the instruction is "to be renewed." It is a present infinitive (the other two are aorists stressing punctiliar
action) and emphasizes the need of being continually renewed.
Now this renewal is to occur "in the spirit of your mind." This
is not a direct reference to the Holy Spirit, for He is never
described with such defining words as here. Rather, Paul refers
to the regenerated human spirit which uses man's mind as its
instrument. Man's God-consciousness, having been made alive
in Christ, governs his mental life, which in turn controls his
actions.

Eadie explains: "The renewal takes place not simply in the
mind, but in the spirit of it. . . . The mind remains as before,
both in its intellectual and emotional structure—in its memory
and judgment, imagination and perception. These powers do
not in themselves need renewal, and regeneration brings no
new faculties. The organism of the mind survives as it was,

but the spirit, its highest part, the possession of which distinguishes man from the inferior animals, and fits him for receiving the Spirit of God, is being renovated. The memory, for example, still exercises its former functions, but on a very different class of subjects; the judgment still discharging its old office, is occupied among a new set of themes and ideas; and love, retaining all its ardour, attaches itself to objects quite in contrast with those of its earlier preference and pursuit."‡

The final infinitive naming what Christians have been taught in Christ (4:21) is "to put on" the new man (v. 24). This is the positive act of which "put off" (v. 22) was the negative. Although Colossians 2:9-10 indicates that this transaction took place at conversion, Paul in Ephesians is explaining the need for a practical display of this spiritual fact.

By receiving Christ, the believer is expected to exhibit Christlikeness. The new man that the believer has become (in contrast to the "old man"—the natural self received from Adam) was created "after God" or more literally, "in accord with God." Just as Adam was created in the likeness of God, so the new creation was likewise in conformity with God. The new man was created "in righteousness and holiness." The first term denotes that which follows the "right" and receives God's approval. The second describes the quality of piety, the reverencing of God's standards and avoidance of the pollutions of sin. "Of the truth" (not simply the adjectival "true" holiness of KJV) applies to both righteousness and holiness, and is in contrasting parallel to "of deceit" in 4:22. That which God has made of us corresponds to truth, the very opposite of the character of sin which dominated the old man.

SPECIFIC INSTRUCTIONS EXPLAINED (4:25—5:21)

The principles of the new life having been set forth, Paul now applies them to specific situations.

‡ John Eadie, *Commentary on the Epistle to the Ephesians,* p. 343.

LYING (4:25)

Putting off the old man (4:22) involves the putting off of lying. By embracing the truth of God, believers have renounced the principle of deceitfulness and the conduct which reflects it. Christians are continually to speak truth. This quotation from Zechariah 8:16 lays upon God's people the perpetual obligation to be truthful. Neither extenuating circumstances nor situational factors relieve them from this obligation. Paul differs from pagan moralizers and mere human pragmatists, however, because of the basis on which the command is issued. It is the principle of the believer's union with Christ, and thus his family relationship with all other believers, that provides the motivation for honest dealings. Paul's thought in this passage seems to be restricted to relationships within Christian society.

ANGER (4:26-27)

"Be ye angry, and sin not." Efforts to make the first imperative merely permissive are not satisfactory. It is best to regard both as true commands. There is an anger which is righteous. Christ was angry at times (Mk 3:5). We should be indignant over injustice, sin, blasphemous statements, and so forth. However, the imperative "sin not" which is coupled with the former cautions us against overindulgence even in what started as righteous anger. The exhortation is couched in the words of Psalm 4:4 (LXX version). Because of the human tendency to allow personal vindictiveness to permeate anger, the safeguard here suggested is to put definite limitations of time on the exercise of anger. Resentments are not to be harbored beyond the day in which they begin. It may not always be possible to straighten out the problem with the other person before nightfall, but at the very least one can settle the matter of his own heart attitude before retiring. As the psalmist said in the clause following the one Paul quoted, "Commune with your own heart upon your bed, and be still" (Ps 4:4b).

Anger which is not curbed lays the person open to irrational and evil suggestions, and Satan is quick to grasp the opportunity. Inasmuch as the devil is always on the prowl to capture men (1 Pe 5:8), Christians certainly should not make his efforts any easier. Unrestrained anger does this very thing. It allows Satan to work through the "old man" and entice us to sin because so often our anger is not righteous. When it is merely an emotional outburst, it escapes the control of the mind, and the Spirit which influences it, and it is this which is continually being renewed as believers grow in grace (4:23). The devil needs only the slightest place to begin operations, and from that point is fully able to produce the utmost havoc. How many Christians have lost their testimony as they have allowed the evil one to exploit their anger into the most unseemly viciousness!

STEALING (4:28)

Paul's actual expression is "the one stealing." It is a present participle and can hardly be relegated to the one who "stole" before he was converted. Rather, it seems to depict the continuing practice of pilfering that still characterized some of these Christians. We must recognize that many of the early Christians came from the ranks of slaves, where pilfering was a way of life. Conversion does not remove all such habits instantaneously, especially in matters where no great conscience has developed.

Furthermore, let us recognize that stealing in the broad sense is not unknown among present-day Christians. Deans of students in any Christian school can elaborate on this problem at some length. Income tax returns, insurance claims, and examinations in school are only a few examples of situations where Christians are many times less than honest.

The scriptural injunction is not merely that stealing cease, nor even that restitution be made. The Christian principle is laid down that each man should toil honestly at that which is good, not merely to meet his own needs and thus avoid temptation to thievery, but to be able to amass a surplus to help others in need. This is in stark contrast to the prevalent attitude which assumes that one is entitled to the supply of needs, whether or not he wishes to work. By working diligently, the individual removes some of the temptation to steal, and by assisting others in need, he helps remove the temptation from them also.

SPEECH (4:29-32)

The word *corrupt* is used of that which is worthless or useless, as well as that which is rotten or decayed. The former, more general meaning would include the latter, and that seems to be the case here. <u>Not just foul language is prohibited, but any and all use of speech which is of no value</u>. Jesus said, "Every idle word that men shall speak, they shall give account thereof in the day of judgment" (Mt 12:36). The third chapter of James is one of the classic passages in Scripture on the use and the abuse of the tongue. Paul here is in complete agreement. Because such contradictory speech can come from the same mouth (even when that mouth belongs to a Christian), the admonition here is most pertinent.

Instead of using his mouth for worthless speech, the Christian should concentrate on making a positive contribution. Today's English Version renders it this way: "Use only helpful words, the kind that build up and provide what is needed." The Christian should be concerned that his speech builds up rather than tears down, and that it fills needs rather than increases them. The goal is that it will "minister grace" to those who hear. Good speech, just as everything else in the Christian's life, should be under the Spirit's control, and thus it can and should be a means of blessing the lives of others.

"And grieve not the holy Spirit of God." The use of "and" ties this statement to the preceding so as to make it not just a general injunction, but a reminder that failure in the area of proper speech grieves the Spirit who indwells each believer. (Perhaps the apostle means to include also lying, anger, and stealing, along with worthless speech.) There may also be an emphasis on the Spirit as being "holy" (lit., "the Spirit, the holy one"), and thus an indication of why sinful conduct is so unbecoming to Christians.

The Holy Spirit is the one "in whom" these readers were sealed (see Eph 1:13). At regeneration the Spirit begins to indwell each believer and a vital union is established, so that He is in us and we are in Him (Jn 14:16-20). Through this act believers receive the seal of ownership and identification which marks them as God's possession. This is God's guarantee until the final phase of redemption shall occur at the coming of Christ. It is thus not a question of losing the Spirit, but of grieving Him who has done so much and who abides within us.

Negative and positive aspects of Christian conduct are next enumerated, related to the matter of proper speaking. Certain traits need to be put away. *Bitterness* is resentment in the heart. It is the attitude that refuses to make reconciliation with others. This leads naturally to *wrath,* the furious outburst of passion or temper. Such all too frequently settles into the permanent attitude of *anger*. This word differs from the preceding one in denoting the more settled disposition in contrast to the sudden outburst. *Clamour* is the loud outcry. Giving way to bitter feelings and bad temper leads to violent arguments and yelling at one another. Then comes *evil speaking,* the injurious and insulting words which deepen the bitterness and resentment, and start the whole distressing chain once again. The entire course of improper speech and thought must be abandoned, along with all other forms of base conduct (KJV, "malice").

These negative forms of conduct must be replaced with positive Christian virtues. Believers should "be kind" to one another. The word describes a gracious, gentle manner, the very opposite of the attitudes named in verse 31. This kindness must be expressed in such ways as tenderheartedness. The display of sympathy and compassion, as commanded here, assumes a willingness to be understanding of others, patient with them, and ready to put kindness into operation. One important way for this virtue to be displayed is by the continual exercise of a forgiving spirit. This is the opposite of the bitterness, anger, and denunciation previously described (4:31).

When confronting real (or imagined) wrongs done to them by other Christians, believers should demonstrate a forgiving spirit and should remember that all believers are members of the same spiritual family. Another strong incentive for the display of forgiveness is the reminder that God in Christ (not KJV, "for Christ's sake") forgave us. The act of God at Calvary, providing forgiveness in Christ, made possible our being sons of God. Surely we should exhibit the nature of our Father.

LOVE (5:1-2)

Inasmuch as "therefore" introduces the various admonitions in the passage (4:1, 17, 25; 5:15), it appears that these verses should not be attached to the discussion of forgiving in the foregoing paragraph, but regarded as an additional exhortation. Christians are admonished to become imitators of God, particularly in the matter of love. The present tense of "become" (rather than simply "be") suggests that this should be continually and increasingly their experience.

"Imitators" conveys the concept of the Greek term better than merely "followers." This is the only place in the New Testament where we are told to be imitators of God. Believers are told, however, to be imitators of what is good (1 Pe 3:13), of Paul (1 Co 4:16; 11:1), of other godly men (Heb 6:11-12), and of Christ (by implication, 1 Co 11:1). The illustration is not as unrealistic as one might suppose, when Paul reminds his readers that they are "beloved children" of God. Being born again as God's children, partaking of His nature and being the objects of His love, believers should exhibit the family likeness in this matter of love. Jesus said the same thing in Matthew 5:48 (cf. vv. 43-47).

The love here described is that which seeks only what is good for its object. It includes both love for God and love for one's fellows. The believer's life should be characterized by a continual walking in the atmosphere of Christian love. The impetus for such a life is supplied by the action of Christ, the

revealer of God (Jn 1:18), who provides us with the model
to emulate. "As Christ also hath loved you" (the ancient manuscripts vary between "you" and "us" for the pronouns in this
passage) refers to the display of Christ's love for men at
Calvary. On the cross Christ gave Himself for us. "For us"
means more than "for our benefit." The preposition (*huper*)
clearly indicates substitution, and thus the vicarious nature of
His death is here stated.

That the whole Old Testament idea of sacrifice and atonement was in Paul's mind is clear from the following part of
the verse. Christ gave Himself as an offering and a sacrifice.
Sometimes these words appear to be interchangeable, but here
where both are used they would seem to be distinctive. If so,
"offering" probably indicates the nonbloody offerings, and
"sacrifice" designates the slain animals which were sacrificed.
Thus Christ is depicted as the true sacrifice toward which the
whole Old Testament system pointed. "A sweetsmelling savour"
pictures the smoke of the offering as it ascended heavenward
and was an apt symbol of the acceptability of the sacrifice
with God. Thus Christ by His love sacrificed Himself for
man's redemption, and this won the full approval of God. Men
can never duplicate the atoning aspect of Christ's sacrifice,
but they can and must follow after His example in demon-
strating the love of God.

PURITY (5:3-14).

As Christians living in a pagan world, these readers (as well
as present-day believers) were breathing the atmosphere of
ungodliness. They needed to be reminded continually not to
allow the standards of the world around them to provide the
norms for their lives. "Fornication" refers here to unlawful
sexual intercourse generally (sometimes the term has the restricted sense of illicit sex before marriage). The Greco-
Roman world had sunk so low morally that this vice was commonly regarded with indifference, even by those whose standards were high in other respects. Paul allows for no misunder-

standing on this point. It is an evil and he pronounces it so.
"All uncleanness" is literally "uncleanness—every kind of it."
This broadens the previous reference to every conceivable filthy
practice. To the Christian living in the mid-twentieth century,
the relevance of this warning is unmistakable. Human nature
and human society, for all their sophistication, have not changed
morally for the better.

"Covetousness" is sometimes explained here as the greedy
desire of sexual appetite, because of the terms just preceding.
It is true that coveting is often connected with sexual sin in
the Bible (e.g., the tenth commandment: "Thou shalt not covet
thy neighbour's wife"). However, the disjunctive "or" is used
here, suggesting that Paul is naming a different vice. Greed,
with its substitution of material values for spiritual ones,
plagued the early church and pagan society, just as it does ours.

These things should not even be named among Christians,
for they are most unbecoming to those who bear the name of
"separated ones" (i.e., "saints"). The meaning is not that such
vices cannot ever be mentioned for warning purposes or other
legitimate reasons (Paul is doing so himself in this passage).
But these things should be so far removed from Christians that
no intimations or suspicions about their presence need have
cause to be mentioned.

"Filthiness" denotes shamefulness of conduct. "Foolish talking" may take on a sexual coloration from the context, although it does not always denote this. Such traits as buffoonery
and flippancy may be referred to. "Jesting" here is used in a
clearly bad sense. Paul is not denying to the Christian a sense
of humor, nor the gaiety of laughter. Proverbs 17:22 says, "A
merry heart doeth good like a medicine." Paul refers to that
jesting which is not appropriate to Christians—the off-color
joke, the spicy story, and the jesting about the sins of others.

The solution to such displays of impurity is for believers to
devote themselves positively to the "giving of thanks." The
Christian's thanksgiving to God is possible only when he is
conscious of his blessings from God. By continually dwelling

on such things and using his mind and tongue to express his gratitude, he will remove the opportunity for indulgence in these filthy vices.

The author's warning against pagan vices is reinforced by the reminder that sins have consequences. "For this ye know" calls his readers' attention to that which was certainly not new information to them. Literally, the rendering could be: "For this ye know, being aware that . . . ." Paul was not issuing an order which might be obeyed or disobeyed, but was mentioning something they fully understood and admitted.

"Whoremonger" (i.e., fornicator), "unclean person," and "covetous man" name performers of the three vices mentioned in verse 3. All of the terms are written without articles, a grammatical feature which emphasizes the general quality rather than particular instances. Thus his thought is not that no person who has ever committed such an act is barred from participation in Christ's kingdom (for the Bible speaks of many who have had such sins forgiven). Rather, he means the person whose life is characterized by this. (In the same way the Bible denounces "rich men" in the strongest terms, but this does not mean that only poor men can be saved. It does mean that if a rich man is to be saved, God's assessment of such a man must enable Him to see him not as a "rich man" but as a repentant sinner who trusts Christ.)

When God looks at a person, He does not view such sins lightly. We see in the "new morality" of our day a tremendous growth of the philosophy that sexual purity is an outmoded concept, and that since sexual desires are natural, satisfaction of them by virtually any means is no longer a moral question. It should be clear from such passages as this that the early church faced precisely the same problems, but that the Word of God speaks to the issue with unmistakable meaning.

Just as in verse 3, "covetous man" is sometimes interpreted narrowly to mean "sexually greedy." The Jerusalem Bible, for example, translates it as "indulges . . . in promiscuity." However, for the reasons suggested in treatment of verse 3, it seems better to treat the word as "covetous" or "greedy," and regard the concept as broad enough to include sexual greed and other things as well. "Who is an idolater" is the King James rendering of a phrase in which the best manuscripts have a neuter pronoun "which." Paul probably means that the whole situation just mentioned constitutes men as idolaters, for they place sensual pleasures and temporal concerns in the forefront of their lives, and devote themselves with their passions to these instead of to God.

When God looks at men and characterizes them with the terms here mentioned, they have no share in the kingdom of Christ and God. The naming of both Christ and God in this way (with the Greek article before the first term but not the second) associates these terms in the closest possible connection. If Christ were not Deity, this juxtaposition would be incongruous.

The fact, however, that this is God's view of sin does not mean that there are not many voices raised in opposition. Many are the self-styled religious experts who deceive the gullible with empty words. Rejecting the revelation of God, they blunt the severity of God's truth and gloss over the fact of coming judgment. Paul reminds us that God's wrath is on the way against such sins as here described. "Sons of " (see also 2:2) is a frequent Hebrew way of referring to a person's characteristics. Thus "sons of disobedience" are those whose lives are characterized by disobedience to God's revealed will. God's wrath will someday fall on them in its full force. It is sometimes said that God hates the sin but not the sinner. Nevertheless, it must not be forgotten that when God's wrath falls, it will fall upon the sinner.

"Be not ye therefore partakers with them" (5:7) can be understood as "Stop becoming partners with them." There is an ever present danger of lapsing into the practices of the old life of disobedience. All Christians need to be on their guard. Now that the Ephesians had trusted Christ, they were to cease their indulging in the same vices.

Paul reminds them of the great change that had occurred when they became Christians. Once they had been "darkness." He does not merely say they had been "in darkness," but that they "were darkness." In their unconverted state they had been so permeated by the realm of evil that they themselves personified that realm. Now as a result of regeneration, they were not only "in the light," but through their vital union with Christ, who is the light of the world, they themselves are here characterized as "light." They share Christ's life and nature and exhibit His character. Believers are the light of the world (Mt 5:14) because Christ is in them (Jn 8:12). The use of the symbols of light and darkness to depict the opposing spiritual realms of God and the evil one is frequent in Scripture and contemporary literature (1 Jn 1:5-6). Paul's readers would have been well acquainted with such terminology.

This abrupt change obligated them to "walk as children of light." Conduct should flow from nature. In the New Testament, Christians are constantly urged to bring their daily walk into line with their position in Christ.

Verse 9 should be set off by dashes or parentheses. The preferred reading replaces "Spirit" (KJV) with "light." The meaning is that the realm of spiritual light in which believers live produces certain results. No verb appears in the sentence, but "is" should be understood. It is possible to understand Paul's statement as meaning that the spiritual product of the realm of light consists of goodness, righteousness, and truth. However, there are easier ways to say this, so that it is more likely that Paul is naming the sphere in which a godly life will be displayed. Instead of conduct which moves in the realm of pagan vices, the Christian life exhibits itself in an atmosphere of goodness, righteousness, and truth. "Goodness" speaks of moral excellence; "righteousness" is rightness as God views it; "truth" is the opposite of all that is false.

Verse 10 is dependent on the verb "walk" in verse 8. "Proving" denotes the action of testing so as to approve what is proper. As a child of the light, the believer is to examine all of his thoughts, words, and deeds in order to bring his life into a continual conformity to the will of God. In this way he will walk in a manner "well pleasing" (better than just "acceptable," KJV) to God.

"Have no fellowship with the unfruitful works of darkness" (5:11). This is parallel to the thought of verse 7. The present tense of the verb corresponds to the present tense of "walk" in verse 8. As believers engage continually in the positive enterprise of walking as children of light, the negative side of this is the avoidance of all that belongs to spiritual darkness.

In the apostle's thought, fruit is the product of the spiritual life, but he does not employ this term for the sinful characteristics of the world. The deeds produced by the realm of darkness are called "works" (also in Gal 5:19), but they are "unfruitful" in the sense of furnishing any profit or good to men or to God. With Paul there are not two kinds of fruit. Rather, men's lives produce either spiritual fruit or barren works.

It is not enough merely to abstain from evil practices. Believers are to "reprove them." To be a true follower of Christ is to take a positive stand for purity. Evil practices are not to be ignored or tolerated, but exposed and attacked for what they are. Jesus called His followers "the salt of the earth" (Mt 5:13), and the primary significance of this metaphor connoted the common retardant against corruption. Christians dare not be so cloistered that they raise no voice against the evils of the day. It should be clear to all whose lives we touch that our standards are those of God's Word, not those of the world of darkness.

Verse 12 remarks that among the works of darkness are some that are done in secret of which it is a shame even to speak. The connection of this verse to the preceding offers some problem. How can one reprove evil works if it is too shameful to speak of them? On the other hand, to explain "reprove" (5:11) as merely the silent rebuke of a pure life does not seem to convey the author's intention. Some explain the shame as belonging to the guilty perpetrators, not the speakers, and of course it is a shameful thing for them to have their deeds exposed. Yet the text states that it is a "shame even to speak," thus implying that the speaker is the one involved. Inasmuch as Paul himself rebukes foul deeds frequently and in explicit language (e.g., Ro 1), he cannot mean that it is sinful to mention them. The best explanation seems to be that to pure souls who are sensitive to evil, it is offensive to mention some of these deeds, even when Christian duty demands that such be dealt with and rebuked

Verse 13 contains obscurities that challenge the interpreter. He must decide whether the words "make manifest" which occur twice are middle or passive in voice. He must also determine the sense of "light" in its two occurrences. To this writer it seems best to understand the verb and participle forms to be passive, and to expect Paul to have used "light" in the same sense in both instances. Thus the first clause reads, "But all things that are reproved by the light are made manifest." The "all things" are the unfruitful works of darkness which the children of light are to reprove (5:11). As believers bring the light of Christ and of God's Word to focus on the shameful deeds of the wicked, their wickedness is clearly seen. It is the nature of light to dispel darkness.

The second clause should read, "For everything which is made manifest is light." Certainly Paul does not mean that shameful deeds will be made respectable. Nor does changing the sense of "light" into the general sense of disclosure provide any aid, because the statement would be redundant (i.e., "Everything which is made manifest is disclosed"). It is best to understand that when Paul speaks of evil deeds being reproved by the light, he means not merely that such are revealed in their wickedness but that the light also serves to correct the problem. In this context (5:8) it has already been mentioned that the readers had experienced this very thing. They had once been darkness, but had been made light by application of the gospel of Christ to them. Thus in Paul's mind is the subjective response to the reproof of sin from God's Word.

A similar idea is expressed in John 3:20-21, "Every one that doeth evil hateth the light, neither cometh to the light, lest his deeds should be reproved. But he that doeth truth cometh to the light, that his deeds may be made manifest, that they are wrought in God." One notices that also in the John passage, "reproof" involves acceptance of the light, while those who remain in the darkness are not reproved.

This section on purity is concluded by an apparent quotation whose source is not entirely certain. Many feel that Paul is quoting from an ancient Christian hymn, largely because of the rhythmical character of the clauses. "He saith" would then be rendered "it says." However, it seems more likely that Paul is citing rather freely the gist of several Old Testament passages, particularly Isaiah 60:1; 52:1-2; and 26:19, with "Christ" substituted for "Jehovah" (60:1). The point of the statement is clear enough: Christians need to be spiritually alert and active, trusting Christ to continue granting them the light they need to walk in purity.

WISDOM (5:15-21).

There is a variation in the word order of verse 15 among the various manuscripts. In some the adverb "accurately" or "carefully" goes with the verb "see," and in others it belongs with the verb "walk." In the former (which seems to be slightly better attested), the sense is, "Look carefully how you are walking." If this be the correct text, then Paul is urging the Ephesians to pay careful attention to their Christian conduct. In the other arrangement of words, the meaning is, "See then how accurately ye are walking." Ultimately the meaning is not much different; either way Paul is telling his readers that their Christian walk deserves the most careful examination, that it might be pleasing to God. The latter order, however, may connote the idea that Paul is not questioning the direction of their walk but its degree of accuracy. As Christians they were heading toward the right goal, but it is possible that they were not all walking as wisely as they might.

"Not as unwise but as wise" explains what sort of walk Paul expects the Christian to maintain. A walk that is careful and accurate is a wise walk, based on that store of spiritual knowledge which God has provided for believers (Eph 1:8). It will draw on the knowledge of God's will which has been revealed in Scripture (1:9) and will put that knowledge into operation in daily life. Such a life is wise, as it accepts the truth which God has revealed and sees the need of bringing the life into conformity to God's desire (2:10).

A wise walk will be "redeeming the time." The expression is literally "buying up the season." The point is that Christians need to employ their spiritual knowledge so as to grasp every opportunity for fulfilling Christian duty and displaying spiritual fruit. "Buying up" suggests paying the necessary price in time and effort. "Season" is that word of time which denotes the appropriate time, time with special characteristics. Believers must be sensitive to the opportunities and circumstances which life affords for manifesting Christian virtues "because the days are evil." "Evil" does not mean difficult or troublesome, but morally corrupt. In a world at enmity with God, every Christian needs to grasp the opportunities which are available to do good. The blacker the night, the more important is the light. Implicit in the statement may be the prospect of impending persecution on a much greater scale, and thus the need to seize every remaining chance before such opportunities are gone.

"Wherefore" (5:17) is literally "on account of this," and is based on the commands in verses 8 and 15 to walk as children of light and walk in wisdom. "Be ye not unwise" emphasizes the senselessness of conduct which is contrary to the will of God. The senselessness of pagan conduct is due to the fact that such persons have no understanding of God's will. Believers, however, may act in accord with knowledge, for they possess in Scripture the objective revelation of God's will and the indwelling Spirit to interpret it to them. The Spirit of God will assist the submissive believer in applying the revelation of God's will to the circumstances of life. When Paul here commands his readers to "understand what the will of the Lord is," it is very evident that he did not regard the Christian life to be devoid of intellectual content. The Christian faith involves vastly more than an emotional experience. Christians are called on to use their mental capabilities to the fullest extent for the highest of all goals—the comprehension of and response to the will of God.

"And be not drunk with wine" (5:18). It is not wine alone that is castigated but drunkenness with wine. It is easily understandable that this must have been a very common sin in Paul's day, when wine was almost universally employed as a beverage. "Excess" is the strong term which depicts dissoluteness, debauchery, dissipation, or incorrigibility. The removal of inhibitions by the use of intoxicants leads to even worse displays of evil.

On the contrary, the Christian is commanded to "be filled with the Spirit." The present tense of the imperative verb makes this a continuing obligation for believers. Now, the Bible never commands Christians to be baptized by the Spirit or to be indwelt by the Spirit. Both are actions which God performs when men trust Christ for salvation. But believers are commanded to be filled with the Spirit, and we find the same Christians being "filled with the Spirit" on more than one occasion (see Ac 2:4; 4:31). We must not imagine some sort of physical entry. This is descriptive language which pictures the control of the person by the Holy Spirit. There is a certain analogy in this contrast between being drunk with wine and being filled with the Spirit. In both instances, the individual is under the control of another influence. The former controls him for evil purposes; the latter for the doing of God's will.

Harry A. Ironside has reminded us of an interesting set of parallels which suggest the meaning of being filled with the Spirit.§ In Ephesians 5:19, the results of filling by the Spirit are set forth as "speaking to yourselves in psalms and hymns

§ H. A. Ironside, *In the Heavenlies*, pp. 269-70.

and spiritual songs." In Colossians 3:16 exactly the same results are mentioned as occurring when "the word of Christ" dwells richly in believers. Ironside points out that in some sense the word of Christ and the Spirit are equal. Therefore, if one would be Spirit-filled, he should allow nothing in his life to be contrary to the Scripture.

Verses 19-21 contain four coordinate participles which show the way in which being "filled with the Spirit" should express itself. The first of these is "speaking to yourselves in psalms and hymns and spiritual songs." "Yourselves" should be understood here as the reciprocal "one another," because Paul is not referring to private meditation but to the believers' relations with each other. Instead of the drunken songs indulged in by pagans when the wine flowed freely, the Christians had a new song which should replace the bawdy ballads of the past.

Efforts to make rigid distinctions among three types of songs seem fruitless. At best one may merely suggest what the differences may have been. "Psalms" may possibly refer to Old Testament psalms set to music, perhaps with instrumental accompaniment. "Hymns" could denote Christian songs of praise to God. "Spiritual songs" employs a more general term for all kinds of songs, with the restriction "spiritual" limiting the reference to those odes which were prompted by the Holy Spirit within the believer. Singing has been a recognized part of Christian worship and devotion from apostolic times. Not only do we find such mentions as this in the New Testament, but also in the report of Pliny regarding the Christians in Bithynia (A.D. 112), and in the writings of Tertullian, also in the second century. Singing the praises of God is a most appropriate response of God's children as they reflect on the salvation He has provided.

"Singing and making melody in your heart to the Lord" is the second way in which Spirit-controlled persons express themselves. If "heart" is instrumental, then the phrase describes the various songs as originating in the heart, not just the formality of the lips. If, however, "heart" is locative, then it describes the unvoiced praise of meditation and worship which is basic to valid outward expression. The former phrase depicts the believers' spiritual communication with one another. This phrase describes the inward spiritual communion of the believer and his Lord.

"Giving thanks always for all things" is the continuing obligation of every believer. Here it is stated as one of the marks of the Spirit-filled man. It involves the continual recognition of the blessings one has received. Such an attitude is easier to talk about or admire abstractly than it is to practice. "For all things" includes misfortunes as well as obvious blessings. Yet we cannot accuse Paul of glibness or superficiality, for he exemplified this trait most remarkably. He was writing these very words while a prisoner in Rome. He once sang hymns and praised God in a dungeon while his feet were in stocks and his back was lacerated (Ac 16:25). It takes, however, the filling of the Holy Spirit (that is, the submission of the Christian to the Spirit's control) in order to respond to all of life's situations in this manner.

"Submitting yourselves one to another in the fear of God" (the best manuscripts read "Christ" in place of "God"). This phrase closes the preceding discussion, adding a fourth participle to show in what way being filled with the Spirit should express itself. This submission in verse 21 must not be explained as being in contradiction to the passage which follows. When Paul says that Christians should submit to one another, he does not mean, for example, that husbands and wives are to submit to each other, for that would render verse 22 meaningless and destroy the very pattern of authority which he is about to teach. Rather, he is exhorting against a spirit of self-exaltation by anyone in the church. He calls for a recognition of the divinely-established order in human life and in the church, and for each Christian to submit himself to whatever human authority he has been placed under. The next section of the epistle will take up some of the relationships involved.

10

MAINTAIN CHRISTIAN RELATIONSHIPS

5:22—6:9

WIVES AND HUSBANDS (5:22-33)

PAUL'S TRANSITION is so smooth that no verb was employed in the sentence originally. Literally, he wrote, "Wives, to your own hubands." Of course, "submit yourselves" is properly inferred from the preceding verse. In each of the three pairs discussed, the subordinate one is exhorted first.

In this instruction of Christian wives to be submissive to their husbands, Paul is in harmony with the uniform teaching of Scripture (see 1 Pe 3:1-6). The exhortation conveys no disparagement of women, but rather relieves them of responsibilities for which they are not best suited and frees them for the pursuit of their God-given functions. There is no hint of any inferiority except in position. Wives may be the equal of and many times superior to their husbands in intelligence, courage, spirituality, moral discernment, discretion, and in a thousand other ways. Furthermore, as members of the body of Christ they are equal (Gal 3:28). But in the matter of authority and position in the home, the Bible is absolutely clear: the wife is subject to the authority of the husband.

This obligation of wives is lifted to the highest plane by the explanation "as unto the Lord." The meaning goes beyond a comparison: "Obey your husbands as you would obey the Lord." The sense is rather, "Submit to husbands as an act of submission to the Lord." Performance of this Christian duty in the marital realm is actual submission to God, for it accepts the order which He has constituted for the human family.

Verse 23 explains, "For the husband is the head of the wife, even as Christ is the head of the church." Here is a further elaboration of the principle of order which is seen in God's arrangement of things. A similar description occurs in 1 Corinthians 11:2-16 (esp. v. 3). There is no more reason for a wife to chafe under the headship of her husband than for the church to complain against Christ. "Himself being Saviour of the body" (lit.). This phrase refers to Christ, who in His position as head of the church is also its Saviour ("body" here is the church, the body of Christ). It may be that Paul has added this assertion to indicate one great respect in which Christ is not analogous to husbands. However, it is possible that he may be drawing at least a slight comparison. Just as Christ is the Saviour of His church, so the husband is to be the protector and physical preserver of his wife. Headship and authority carry responsibility with them. Recognition of this on the part of wives makes compliance more palatable.

Verse 24 in the Greek text begins with the strong adversative "but" (not "therefore," KJV), and this has given rise to several explanations as to the logical connection with what precedes. Some suppose a suppressed thought here: "Do not disobey your husbands, *but* as the church is subject unto Christ, so let the wives be to their husbands in everything." It may be more likely that Paul is guarding against a wrong conclusion being drawn from his previous statement. In spite of the fact that Christ as Saviour is different from the earthly husband's headship, the truth of obedience being illustrated is not affected. In every lawful thing pertaining to the marriage relation, wives are to obey their husbands in the same manner as the church is expected to obey Christ. As a matter of fact, the two are related, for by the Christian wife's obedience to her husband she is also acting in obedience to this precept of Christ as a part of His church. Paul has provided the highest of motivations and analogies to assist Christian wives in their marital responsibilities.

The apostle then turns in verses 25-33 to the duties of the Christian husband. It is summed up by the opening statement, "Husbands, love your wives." Although he has told the wives to be in subjection, he does not tell the husbands to treat their wives as subjects. How often trouble comes when the specific admonitions of Scripture are appropriated by the wrong parties. This injunction of Paul provides an answer to possible problems arising from the previous instruction to wives. No normal wife resents her husband's headship, provided that his love for her is what it should be.

The very highest ideal is set before the husband. He is to love his wife "even as Christ also loved the church." Such a standard obviously rules out all brutality. No place remains here even for a patronizing air, or lack of consideration. The love enjoined is not conjugal love, but the same sort of attitude which God displayed in saving men (Jn 3:16), and which He continues to bestow on His children (Jn 14:21, 23). On the other hand, it means that a husband cannot love his wife "too much" (one may love unwisely, but never too much), for the standard is Christ's love for His church.

The particular feature of this love which the apostle emphasizes is its self-sacrificing character. He reminds his readers how Christ gave Himself for His church. This example of the highest love was mentioned also by Jesus shortly before the crucifixion when He gave His new commandment to His disciples: "Love one another, as I have loved you. Greater love hath no man than this, that a man lay down his life for his friends" (Jn 15:12-13). When husbands love their wives to this extent, they usually find no problem in being the head of the home.

Verse 25 states what Christ did for His church in the past, when He gave Himself for her redemption. Verse 26 names Christ's present purpose and activity for the church. He gave Himself in order that He might sanctify the church. His purpose was to make possible a company of people who are separated to Him and cleansed from sin in their lives. The verb "sanctify" is probably constative, looking at the entire present life of the church. "Cleanse" is an aorist participle (constative also), and describes how the sanctifying is effected: "That He might sanctify it, by cleansing. . . ."

This cleansing is accomplished "by the washing of the water in the word." In spite of some attempts to explain *loutrōi* as "laver," the term more likely refers to a bath or washing, rather than the place of washing. Many regard this "washing of the water" as a direct reference to baptism. However, this washing is stated to be that cleansing in which the instrument is located in the Word. The Word of God is the cleansing agent for this present aspect of sanctification, in which the church already forgiven by the atonement is being progressively made pure in practice by the application of God's Word. The particular term for "word" here (*rhēmati*) emphasizes a spoken utterance. We are reminded of the words of Jesus, "Now ye are clean through' the word which I have spoken unto you" (Jn 15:3). The Word of God spoken by Jesus and recorded as Scripture (and preached to men) is Christ's instrument to cleanse His church from sinful defilement. The Word of God sets forth the standards of divine righteousness and acts as the instrument to probe and convict and to cause repentance, confession, and rectification.

Verse 27 explains Christ's ultimate purpose for the church. The present aspect of sanctification described in the previous verse has a goal which shall be realized when Christ and His church shall be finally united in the fullest sense for all eternity. The comparison of Christ and the church to a husband and his bride is here extended to the final presentation of the bride to her bridegroom. Normally in the custom, the bride is presented to her bridegroom by a third party (see 2 Co 11:2 for Paul's use of the same verb "present"). Regarding the church, however, it is Christ who presents the church to Himself, for He is the only one who could prepare her for this occasion.

"Not having spot or wrinkle or any such thing." "Spot" is something splashed on from without; "wrinkle" would be a fault in her own body. R. C. H. Lenski says, "The world about the church causes the stains, the flesh still in her causes the wrinkles."* But at Christ's coming, the church will be "holy and without blemish." These terms are literal ("spot or wrinkle" are figurative). The complete transformation of the church will occur only when we see Christ.

Although verses 25b-27 may be regarded as something of a digression, as Paul having mentioned Christ and the church pauses to recount the great program that has been planned for believers, it surely is also a delineation of the greatness of Christ's love for His church. It was this love which prompted Him to give Himself, and then to continue His program of present sanctification until the glorious future when, as the Bridegroom, He comes to claim His bride. Such love provides the most sublime ideal to which husbands can be pointed for guidance in their relationships with their wives.

At verse 28 Paul draws the conclusion from the preceding illustration. Husbands ought to love their own wives as their own bodies. As the church is the body of Christ, so the wife is here regarded as the body of her husband. "As their own bodies" does not mean that men should love their wives "as though they were their own bodies" or "as much as they do their own bodies," but "as constituting their own bodies." This is made clear by the remainder of the verse, as well as by the analogy of Christ and the church. Christ loves the church "as constituting" His body. The husband should do likewise. As the two have become one in marriage, the wife has become part of her husband. Thus the conclusion Paul draws is sound: "He who loves his wife loves himself." This love is therefore not merely an obligation, but a response based on the very nature of the relationship.

To emphasize just how normal this should be, Paul cites

* R. C. H. Lenski, *The Interpretation of St. Paul's Epistles to the Galatians, to the Ephesians, and to the Philippians*, p. 635.

the general principle, "No one ever hated his own flesh" (although as Eadie remarks, "fools and fanatics excepted"†). Suicide is always recognized as abnormal behavior. The normal pattern is for a person to nourish and cherish his body. People go to great effort and expense to care for the needs and comforts of their own bodies, and this Paul fully assumes and approves. Inasmuch as the wife is one flesh with her husband, and thus is regarded as his body, she is to be nourished and cherished. Once again Paul reminds his readers of how Christ nourishes and cherishes His church. Christ's loving care for the church is recognized and enjoyed by every believer. He provides spiritual food, temporal blessings, and has assumed responsibility for supplying all needs (Phil 4:19). He functions as the head of the church, and exercises all the duties which headship demands. Furthermore, He does it with loving grace, never with threats or brutality. The analogy to the subject at hand is a good one, "for we are members of his body" (5:30), just as husbands and wives are one flesh. (The clause, "of his flesh and of his bones," is apparently an interpolation from Gen 2:23, and is dropped from most Greek texts today. Its inclusion adds nothing vital to the sense, and has given rise to certain forced interpretations.)

To provide the scriptural basis for this teaching, Paul quotes Genesis 2:24, spoken by Adam following the creation of Eve. Some have attempted to allegorize this statement as used in Ephesians, referring it to Christ ("a man") and the church ("his wife"). It has been referred to the incarnation and to the second coming. However, the difficulty with "mother" in the analogy makes such attempts seem forced if not actually crude.

It is much more likely that Paul uses the quotation in its normal sense of human marriage. The quotation makes the point that God created the sexes in order to establish in marriage the closest of human unions. Prior to marriage, the closest

† John Eadie, *Commentary on the Epistle to the Ephesians*, p. 424.

ties are with one's parents. From the time of marriage, however, there is no question but that a man's strongest and closest tie must be with his wife. Sexual union unites husband and wife as one flesh in the most intimate way. Yet this is merely the physical aspect of this union, and there are many other ways in which the relationship of true marriage forms the strongest and most enduring of human ties. As dearly as one may love and respect his parents, marriage creates a new and higher allegiance which supersedes the former one. Brides and bridegrooms must recognize this and be willing to "leave" father and mother. Until they are ready to do this, they are not mature enough for marriage. Anything which disrupts this closest of unions is a violation of God's intention since creation.

"This mystery is great" (5:32). This is a most difficult verse to interpret with due regard for its contextual connections. Verses 28-31 have been speaking of human marriage (except for the brief reference to Christ in 5:29b-30), so that one would expect verse 32 also to refer to marriage. Yet Paul specifically says, "But I speak concerning Christ and the church." Then in verse 33 he speaks of marriage again. The alternative, which regards verse 31 as an allegorical description of Christ and the church, has been discussed above and its weaknesses noted.

The best explanation would appear to be as follows. The revealed truth (i.e., "mystery") regarding marriage is of profound importance ("great"). Marriage, however, pictures an even greater union—the union between Christ and the church, and it is the recognition of this union which provides for Christians the concept that gives the richest meaning to domestic life.

Paul began this discussion with marriage, and brought in Christ and the church as an illustration and incentive (5:23). Now as he nears the close of this subject, he uses the passage on marriage in Genesis 2 as the illustration of the mystical union with Christ. We may note, however, that there is a vital connection between these concepts. Inasmuch as Paul is addressing Christian husbands and wives, they are involved not only in the truth revealed by God about the purposes and results of marriage, but also in the deeper truth regarding the union of Christian believers (i.e., the church) with Christ. They are members of the church as well as partners in a marriage.

"Nevertheless let every one of you in particular so love his wife" (5:33). Paul does not lose himself in his illustration about Christ. He brings his readers back to the practical consideration of human marriage with which he began the discussion (v. 22). The emphasis in the first part of the verse is on each husband individually. He is to love his wife "as himself." This means not "as he loves himself," but "as being part of himself." The central point made in the previous verses is that husbands and wives are one. Hence the love here expected is derived from the very nature of the relationship.

Likewise the wife is again enjoined to reverence her husband. The verb employed is commonly translated "fear," but is used here as frequently elsewhere in the sense of "respect." This summarizes what was said in verses 22-24. In the similar passage in 1 Peter 3:1-6, such respectful conduct on the part of wives is said to be the finest adornment of the Christian woman and constitutes her a true daughter of the Old Testament Sarah.

Although Paul has sometimes been accused of an uncharitable attitude toward women, a careful study of his writings exonerates him from this charge. Wherever Christianity has gone (and the writings of Paul have been prominent in its advance), it has elevated the status of women. Even though instances of domestic living on a very high moral plane can be shown from history, these were by no means the general rule. The fact that passages appear such as Colossians 3:18-19, 1 Peter 3:1-7, and this one in Ephesians 5, shows how important this instruction was and perhaps how much it was needed. Even today, missionaries report that many areas of the world where the gospel has not penetrated deeply have little or no concept of God's ideal for the family. Marital infidelity and brutal treatment of wives are commonplace. Sad to say, these things still exist among those who possess God's truth and claim to have committed themselves to Christ. There is a great need for the display of Christian standards in every Christian home.

CHILDREN AND PARENTS (6:1-4)

From the basic relation of husband and wife, Paul moves to the relation of children and their parents. As in the former instance, he begins with the subordinate party. Children are exhorted to obey their parents. We note that both parents are included. Mother, as well as Father, is to be obeyed. Scripture places much stress on obedience to parents, and the current lack of it in many quarters is surely the cause of much juvenile delinquency. Yet this has always been the case. It was a contributing cause of the depravity in the pagan world (Ro 1:30) and will characterize the last days (2 Ti 3:2). "In the Lord" belongs with the verb "obey," and describes the sphere in which this obedience is expected. Paul is addressing Christian families. He is not discussing the problem of believing children with unbelieving parents, and thus does not take up the unfortunate cases where parents demand conduct contrary to the will of God.

Obedience to parents is declared to be "right." This is not only because it is "proper" in a general sense as recognized by almost all cultures, but because it is "righteous," according to God's Word which commands it.

Paul quotes the fifth commandment of the Decalogue (Ex 20:12), which enjoined children to honor their parents. "Honor" goes beyond obedience to the attitude of heart which produces obedience. The rendering "which is the first commandment with promise" (KJV) has caused certain difficulties. It has been pointed out that the second commandment (Ex 20:5-6) has promises attached. If one views the elaboration of the second commandment as a description of the nature of God rather than as specific promises to keepers of a particular precept, then he is faced with the problem that the fifth commandment is the *only* one of the Decalogue with a promise, not just the *first*. It may be that "first" should be regarded as "foremost," and thus the sense would be: "A commandment of primary importance and also accompanied by a promise." However, there is no compelling reason why Paul cannot be understood as meaning that the commandment to honor parents is the first one with a promise of blessing attached (understanding the second commandment as explained above), even though many later commands in the Mosaic legislation also contained promises.

The particular promise involved spiritual prosperity ("it may be well with thee") and temporal prosperity as well. Another Pauline statement regarding the twofold benefit of godly living is 1 Timothy 4:8, "Godliness is profitable unto all things, having promise of the life that now is, and of that which is to come." Eadie remarks: "We understand the command, as modified by its Christian and extra-Palestinian aspect, to involve a great principle, and that is, that filial obedience, under God's blessing, prolongs life, for it implies the posssession of principles of restraint, sobriety, and industry, which secure a lengthened existence."‡

At verse 4 Paul addresses "fathers" in relation to their children. Although it is true that the same word is used sometimes in the sense of "parents" (e.g., Heb 11:23), it is not likely that it is so used here, inasmuch as "father" was used in its usual sense just two verses earlier. The mention of "fathers" does not relieve mothers from acting as supervisors of their children also, but it does indicate the fathers as heads of their households on whom the ultimate responsibility for supervision rests.

"Provoke not your children to wrath." The present tense of

‡ Ibid., p. 442.

the verb prohibits the continual arousing to anger. It is a warning against the sort of iron-handed discipline that eventually breaks the spirit of a child (see Col 3:21). Unjust demands, unreasonable severity, and unremitting criticism produce bitterness instead of training. That is not to say that permissiveness is what Paul enjoins. Rear them, he says, "in discipline and instruction of the Lord." "Discipline" implies training in proper conduct, and chastening in times of failure. "Instruction" involves teaching, whether by praise, warning, censure, or explanation of principles. As fathers (and mothers) rear their children, they must not neglect the spiritual aspects of their education. All of their dealings with their children should be in accord with the Lord's standards as revealed in Scripture. Parents can give their children no better preparation for life than to provide them with a thorough awareness of and respect for the righteous precepts of the Lord. "The fear of the LORD is the beginning of wisdom" (Pr 9:10).

SLAVES AND MASTERS (6:5-9)

The "servants" (KJV) mentioned in this passage were actually slaves. Because such a large proportion of the Roman Empire consisted of slaves, it is likely that the proportion in the church was large also. This social phenomenon contained the seeds of many conflicts for the church; perhaps the greatest of these occurred when both master and slave were Christians. The proclamation that in Christ there is neither "slave nor free man" (Col 3:11; Gal 3:28) must have caused many a disapproving glance by a slave toward his master.

Yet the Bible neither condones slavery nor advocates its violent overthrow. Even though the New Testament lays down principles which eventually undermined the system, this was a by-product. The main thrust of the biblical teaching is that every man should live righteously in whatever circumstances he may be.

By describing the masters as "according to the flesh," Paul not only identifies them as human (in contrast to their divine

Master), but may be reminding these Christian slaves of the comparatively temporary nature of this slavery, confined as it is to this life. There may also be the hint that their present servitude is only with respect to their physical life. Even now their spirits enjoyed the liberty that is found in Christ.

They must serve, however, "with fear and trembling." This need not refer to an abject dread of their masters, but rather to an earnest zeal in discharging their duties. Paul used the same expression to describe his own preaching (1 Co 2:3) and to describe Christian conduct (2 Co 7:15; Phil 2:12). Their service was to be with "singleness of your heart, as unto Christ." It was not to be halfhearted or hypocritical, but exercised with the consciousness that Christ Himself is served when believers faithfully perform even mundane obligations.

They must avoid "eyeservice," working only when the master's eye is on them. Such falseness would constitute them as "menpleasers," those who fawningly appear to be faithful when in reality they are not. Rather, they must regard themselves as "slaves of Christ," obligated to serve Him with all their energies. This is every Christian's primary allegiance, which ennobles all lesser servitude. Since the Christian slave actually is Christ's servant, he is obligated to carry out this order of his Lord which requires him to serve his earthly master faithfully. This service for his master in the flesh becomes the "will of God" for him, and he should perform it with wholeheartedness and devotion. For the Christian slave in the first century, doing the will of God meant being the best possible Christian slave.

Verse 7 reminds the slave that his service should be performed with "good will." The term implies zeal and enthusiasm. No sullenness or grudging service, whether prompted by an unsympathetic pagan master or by a Christian owner who did not free his slaves, should characterize the conduct of the Christian slave.

A twofold incentive is held out to the slave. He is to remember who his true Lord is, and he is reminded of his ultimate reward. "As to the Lord" suggests at first reading that the slave should work for his master as though he were Christ Himself. However, there may be an even stronger implication. The slave should serve his earthly master faithfully because such service actually is performing the will of God (6:6), and it is the Lord who will reward (v. 8). In a similar passage Paul states, "Ye serve the Lord Christ" (Col 3:24). Thus the slave is freed from feelings of degradation, for his service is shown to be as honorable as any other.

The early manuscripts vary at verse 8 between "whatsoever good thing any man doeth" (KJV) and "if he shall do any good thing," although the sense is not greatly affected. The point in either reading is that the Christian slave can expect proper recognition at the hands of his heavenly Master. Even though an earthly master might not always give credit where such was due, faithful service would not be wasted, for the Lord is mindful of all the actions of all His servants. Hence lack of appreciation by an ungracious master was no excuse for bitterness, for the day of final reckoning still lay ahead. This principle of ultimate reward from God holds good for all, "whether slave or freeman." God evaluates the Christian conduct of all His children, and in His grace He will reward His servants at the judgment seat of Christ, in ways far more significant and enduring than could any earthly benefactor.

Social slavery no longer exists in America, nor in most other parts of the world. The principles of conduct set forth here, however, are applicable to all who are in positions of subordination. If slaves were required by Scripture to give energetic and faithful service in spite of frequently oppressive circumstances, how much more are present-day employees bound to give an honest day's work in conditions far more congenial to their well-being. How much greater blame rests on the employee whose labor brings reproach to the gospel and to Christ, as compared to the slave of ancient times.

Paul's instructions to slaveowners were equally pointed (6:9). The slaveowners in view were undoubtedly Christians, since Paul had no opportunity to exhort any other kind in this letter. In urging them to "do the same things" to their slaves, he surely did not mean that the masters were to obey commands from their slaves, but rather that they were to exhibit the same good will (v. 7) and Christian principles as their slaves.

At the same time the masters were to avoid the harshness and threatenings that so characterized most slaveowners. Vile language, threats of extreme violence, and unjust accusations were to be shunned as inconsistent with the Christian commitment of the master. The incentive Paul uses is a reference once again to the person of Christ, our heavenly Master. He is the Lord of both master and slave, and thus both are responsible to Him. His presence in heaven is a reminder to us of who He is—the exalted Son of God who is the observer of all our conduct.

Furthermore, in His position as our Master, He is the one to whom we all are responsible and must eventually give account. In the slave, Christ as Master should inspire faithful service and assure of ultimate reward. In masters, Christ should inspire kind treatment of their subordinates because He will someday judge the masters. And this judgment will be absolutely impartial. Christ will not be swayed by the external factors that often affect justice on earth. "The gold ring of the master does not attract His eye, and it is not averted from the iron fetter of the slave."§ Christ is no more impressed with Christian masters than with Christian slaves. Righteous conduct will be the significant factor, not social standing. These principles apply just as much to Christian employers today as to slaveowners in the past.

§ Ibid., p. 455.

11

STAND FIRM IN SPIRITUAL CONFLICT

6:10-20

THE CONFLICT (6:10-12)

PAUL NOW SHIFTS from exhorting various groups within the church to a closing word of instruction for the congregation as a whole. One of the greatest mistakes any Christian can make is to assume that salvation in Christ brings the cessation of all problems. Christ never promised His followers that discipleship was an easy life. On the contrary, He taught that following Him involves difficulty and suffering. On one occasion He likened it to a king preparing to battle an enemy, and pointed out the importance of knowing accurately one's resources so as to battle successfully (Lk 14:27, 31-33). In this striking paragraph, Paul also discusses the conflict in which the Christian is engaged, and explains the resources which will assure him of victory.

The believer, he says, needs to be empowered in the Lord. He is to let the power of the Lord be exercised in his life (note that the verb is passive, "be empowered"). The nature of the conflict in view is so serious that nothing less than the "power of his might" is sufficient for the Christian. "Power" refers to strength in operation, while "might" is residual, inherent strength. Paul means that the believer needs the operating power of God, drawn from His almighty supply, in order to live victoriously.

Each Christian is to "put on the whole armour of God" (6:11). Paul was writing these words from a Roman prison.

He had seen many a Roman soldier in recent years, and had abundant opportunity to observe their dress, weapons, and preparation for duty. Thus he takes for his illustration a Roman soldier dressing himself for battle with his full equipment. "Whole armour" is one term in the original text—the soldier's panoply, or complete suit of armor. Because the Christian's conflict is so serious, nothing less than the "panoply of God" will suffice. Even a saved man has no inherent defense against Satanic power apart from the armor which God furnishes. Satan has such clever strategems ("wiles" was used also in 4:14 of the strategems employed by deceitful men who are the tools of Satan) to turn believers aside from the truth or cause them to compromise with it that God's armor and inner strengthening are needed in order to "stand firm" without retreating.

Paul wants his readers to make no mistake about the nature of this conflict. It is not a wrestling with flesh and blood (literally, "blood and flesh"). This reference to hand-to-hand combat emphasizes the personal nature of this struggle. Each believer has his own struggle to face. Further, even though men seem often to be the chief enemies of God and His church, Paul indicates that our struggle is not really against unbelieving men. Rather, it is a vital spiritual encounter. It is "against principalities, against powers, against the rulers of the darkness of this world, against spiritual wickedness" (better, "against spiritual forces of wickedness"). Most of these terms are used elsewhere in Scripture to refer to spirit beings (cf. Eph 1:21; Col 1:16). Here Paul has reference to evil spirit beings under Satan's control, which oppose God and God's people and are a real force to be reckoned with.

This conflict between believers and the spiritual forces of wickedness takes place "in the heavenlies." (This is the fifth occurrence of this phrase in Eph. See comments on 1:3). It is the realm where Christ is supreme (1:20), and where believers also share in its blessings because they are united with Christ (1:3; 2:6). However, angelic beings (both good and bad, 3:10; 6:12) presently inhabit this realm also, and during this age warfare is waged between God's own and the followers of Satan. For a glimpse behind the scenes at angelic activity as it affects the world, one should consult Daniel 10. An instance of angelic activity as it may affect individual persons is seen in Job 1:6-22. Paul thus forewarns us that the Christian's basic conflict in the world is a spiritual one, for all of Satan's forces are arrayed against him in order to thwart wherever possible the purposes of God (cf. 2 Co 4:3-6).

THE ARMOR (6:13-17)

In such a conflict as just described, no ordinary weapons will suffice. The believer will need the full armor of God. "Take" (6:13) is the usual term for taking up one's weapons. The picture is of the heavily armed hoplite getting himself dressed for the battle. It should be noted that all the equipment is defensive except for the sword, and of course, it could be used defensively also. Christians are never told to attack Satan, but to withstand or resist him. The idea of "standing firm," not yielding to his blows, is emphasized in this passage by the recurrence of the term "stand" and similar terms in verses 11, 13, and 14. As John Gerstner has so well stated it, when tempted to do wrong, we should flee as Joseph did from Potiphar's wife; but when attacked by Satan for doing right, we should stand firm as Daniel did before the decree of Nebuchadnezzar.*

The "evil day" mentioned here is not some future eschatological era, but denotes that time when Satan attacks with some temptation, discouragement, or other crisis which would entice to sin. There is inevitably an "evil day" for every Christian, and there are probably many such. At these moments, the properly armed Christian can "withstand" all the evil forces arrayed against him, and when he has used the armor as in-

* John H. Gerstner, *The Epistle to the Ephesians*, p. 80.

tended and has finished the battle, he can "stand" in victory (6:13).

The various items of the armor seem to be enumerated in the general order in which a hoplite would dress himself for battle. "Having your loins girt about with truth." The ancient soldier wore a short tunic over which was placed a leather belt or girdle. This served to keep the loose tunic from getting in the way, and also as a place on which to fasten the breastplate and the scabbard for his sword. In like manner the Christian is to be equipped with truth for spiritual conflict. This does not seem to be "the truth," that is, the Word of God, for that is represented by the sword. Rather, it represents the attitude of truthfulness, the honest and sincere handling of our God-given weapons, which must characterize the effective warrior. One cannot hope to grow spiritually and thwart the evil one's attacks if he is not willing to live with absolute truthfulness and integrity. This attitude is the demonstration of his union with Christ who is the truth (Jn 14:6).

The breastplate was attached to the belt and protected the heart and other vital organs. The "breastplate of righteousness" symbolizes righteousness of life, inasmuch as believers are instructed to put it on. (All believers already possess the imputed righteousness of Christ.) Paul seems indebted to Isaiah 59:17 for several of the figures in this series. In all our spiritual battles, we must never descend to carnal methods and thereby lose that personal righteousness which provides an inner bulwark against spiritual collapse. Righteousness of life, made possible by the new life created in us by Christ Jesus, protects us from the spiritual defeats which would surely come from an accusing conscience and an impure life.

"Having shod the feet." The feet are what carry the soldier to the battle. Feet properly shod enable the soldier to march long distances and to fight without slipping or stumbling on rough terrain. Spiritually, the Christian is to be shod with the "preparation of the gospel of peace." He achieves a confident readiness for the conflict through the peace of God provided in the gospel. A recognition that the good news of salvation has provided peace with God and thus all that we need for spiritual victory furnishes us with calmness for the conflict. In spite of outward attack, the sturdy Christian warrior may have inward peace, and thus his feet can march unafraid to the battle.

If these words about the "feet" were suggested to Paul by Isaiah 52:7, there may be another aspect to his concept here. The Old Testament passage states: "How beautiful upon the mountains are the feet of him that bringeth good tidings, that publisheth peace; that bringeth good tidings of good, that publisheth salvation." This passage speaks of those who carry the message of salvation to others. Thus Paul would mean that the Christian warrior must ever be ready to oppose the evil one by carrying the gospel to the lost. This will bring peace to those at enmity with God. It appears to the writer that the former explanation is more in harmony with the context (which speaks of the believer's own readiness to meet the evil day) than an exhortation to evangelize others, unless one is prepared to see in this symbol both a defensive and an offensive piece of armor.

The shield referred to in verse 16 denotes the large device, four feet by two and one-half feet, that covered the front of the soldier. Grasping it with his left hand, he protected himself from the weapons of the enemy. Sometimes arrows were dipped in a burning substance before they were shot, but the heavy leather-covered shield would knock them down and cause them to be extinguished. In like manner the believer needs "the shield of faith" to counteract the "fiery darts of the wicked one." In this expression the objective sense indicated by "the faith" (the original text has the article) appears to coalesce with the subjective sense of personal faith, for the believer is to take up the shield and use it. He is to repose his trust in the body of truth regarding salvation that God has revealed and use it to quench the fiery darts. Inasmuch as these darts of Satan are rendered harmless by the faith exercised by the believer, perhaps the darts represent doubts regarding God's Word. Whenever spiritual conflict brings doubts regarding the Scripture, the believer who knows the truth embodied in God's Word and who places his faith firmly in it is fully protected from the darts of doubt.

The "helmet of salvation" is a figure drawn from the Old Testament (Is 59:17), where Jehovah Himself is so attired. Here Paul tells the believer to "receive the helmet of salvation," using a different word from the "take" of 6:16, and suggestive of the fact that salvation is the gift of God which the believer receives. In 1 Thessalonians 5:8 the helmet is called the hope of salvation to be realized in the future. Salvation is viewed in Scripture from several standpoints. It is past in the sense that believers have already been saved by grace through faith (Eph 2:8). It is future in the sense that its consummation will occur when Christ returns, and this is the Christian's blessed hope (Ro 13:11). It is also a present experience as God progressively sanctifies believers (Phil 2:12-13).

Inasmuch as the past salvation of these Christian warriors is assumed, and the command is to receive the helmet now (not in some eschatological future), the intent of Paul must have centered on the Christian's present experience. The expression is similar to the thought of 1 Timothy 6:12, "Lay hold on eternal life." That salvation which became our possession through faith in Christ, and whose consummation is our glorious prospect, has some very real implications for our present experience. The settled assurance that one is truly saved and cannot be eternally harmed by the adversary is a strong helmet for the head in the time of spiritual battle. It protects against cowardly fear, as we continually remember that salvation is a present possession and a future certainty.

The "sword of the Spirit" is defined by Paul as the Word of God, provided by the Spirit's inspiration and illumination. With it the Christian soldier is able to defend himself against the thrusts of the evil one and also to attack the false teachings which Satan promotes. The greatest example of the Word of God being used to defeat Satan was Jesus Himself in the temptations described in the gospels (e.g., Mt 4:1-11).

The Strategy (6:18-20)

A soldier may have the best of equipment and still be of no help in the battle unless he is deployed at the right place and at the right time. He needs direction as to his particular function in the conflict. Likewise the Christian also must be aware of the spiritual battle strategy so as to contribute his part to the victory.

"Praying always with all prayer and supplication in the Spirit." The believer must keep in constant communication with his Commander in every season of conflict. Only in this way is he enabled to follow the leading of his Master closely. "Prayer" is the more general term for man's worshipful approach to God; "supplication" emphasizes requests or petitions. Praying is to be "in the Spirit," that is, in the energy and with the purposes which the indwelling Holy Spirit prompts within the believer. Such praying will always desire the will of God and will trust Him for the victory.

By prayer the Christian warrior is to be watchful for the needs of other believers in conflict and should intercede with God on their behalf. We have a spiritual obligation to strengthen one another by prayer and encouragement. Some Christians may be in greater need than others, so believers should be spiritually alert (the word *watchful* means "being awake, sleepless") in order to help them in various ways, and particularly by prayer.

Paul asks his readers also to remember him in their praying. He too faces the attack of the enemy and needs the prayer support of others. In particular, he asks "that utterance may be given to me in the opening of my mouth." He needed both opportunity and boldness to bear his testimony in his present circumstances. His opportunities to preach were, of course, greatly altered from former days. By being a prisoner in Rome, he was confined to one location and prevented from making new contacts. Nevertheless, he did see prison guards and visitors from time to time. He wanted to make the most of each of these opportunities. Whenever he opened his mouth to testify of Christ, he wanted to be effective.

It is not unlikely that Paul may have had a special occasion in mind. As he was confined in Rome, he was waiting for the trial which would decide his appeal. At that time he would doubtless be called on to make a statement in his defense. His desire was that there would be no compromise, but a clear pronouncement of the truth in whose cause he had become a prisoner.

Paul wanted "to make known the mystery of the gospel" with boldness. He has previously used the expression *mystery* in Ephesians to refer to the revelation regarding the inclusion of both Gentile and Jew in one new spiritual body, the church (3:3-6). Although it is possible that such is the meaning in verse 19, it seems more probable that Paul has defined "mystery" here by the phrase "of the gospel." This understanding of Paul's statement includes the truth of the former explanation, for the proclamation of the gospel in its fullest sense includes the truth that all believers became part of the church which is Christ's body.

The apostle did not complain about his lot nor ask prayer at this time that he might be freed, but only that he might take fullest advantage of his circumstances to exercise his ministry. He regarded himself literally as "an ambassador with a chain." The chain here was probably a handcuff. (It could hardly have been the heavy fetters of a condemned prisoner, for during this first Roman imprisonment, Paul was not yet convicted. One should note the alarm of the Roman officer who ordered Paul bound and then discovered that he was a Roman citizen, Ac 22:29.) What an anomaly! A handcuffed ambassador! Instead of the respectful and dignified treatment that a representative of a foreign government expects to receive, Paul in representing the Lord Jesus Christ wore the handcuffs of a prisoner. But this never caused him to forget his mission. When he appeared soon before the tribunal which would rule on his release, he wanted an opportunity for a witness to the gospel to be borne.

Part Four

CLOSING SALUTATION

6:21-24

12

FINAL GREETINGS

6:21-24

IN CLOSING THIS LETTER, Paul explains that he will be sending it by his messenger Tychicus, who was also the bearer of the epistles to Philemon and to the Colossians (Col 4:7). It is most probable that all three letters were carried on the same trip.

Tychicus was one of Paul's most trusted colleagues. He was from the province of Asia (Ac 20:4), and could have been from Ephesus, the capital. He had traveled with Paul on the third missionary journey, and presumably accompanied him to Jerusalem with the collection. Now he was at Rome with the apostle, and would have the responsible task of delivering these important letters to their destinations, as well as conducting the runaway slave Onesimus safely to his master in Colosse. Years later he would be sent by Paul to Ephesus once again (2 Ti 4:12). To call him a "beloved brother" was to emphasize Paul's personal attachment to him. To describe him as a "faithful minister" points to his trustworthy performance of spiritual responsibilities. "In the Lord" belongs to both expressions and denotes the spiritual realm in which Paul and Tychicus find the basis for their association.

Tychicus would be able to give the Ephesians (as well as the Colossians) a firsthand account of Paul's current situation. The emphasis on this function as stated and then repeated in verses 21 and 22 suggests both a special interest in Paul

by these readers, and also some particular significance to
Paul's present status. It may be that Paul's expectation of
release from this first Roman imprisonment had reason for
particular optimism at this time. He also includes the circumstances of his other companions as being part of what
Tychicus would report ("our affairs," v. 22). A list of his
companions at this time is given in Colossians 4:10-15. Paul
felt certain that this report would bring comfort, probably in
the sense of encouragement, to their hearts. One of the en-
couraging items at this time was certainly Paul's prospect of
an early release, as he indicated in the letter to Philemon
(Phile 22).

The statement regarding Tychicus is almost word-for-word
the same as Colossians 4:7-8. This is not too surprising when
one recognizes that both epistles were written at virtually the
same time and that Tychicus would be delivering both. One
difference, however, is that Ephesians 6:21 states, "that ye
also may know my affairs," but Colossians 4:8 omits "also."
Some suggest that he wrote Colossians first, and then when he
wrote the similar statement in Ephesians, he said "ye also."
However, unless this be an almost unconscious insertion by
Paul, it would presuppose that the Ephesian readers would
be familiar with the Colossian letter also, and this is unlikely
at its first reading, and it would hardly have been ethical for
Tychicus to have let the Ephesians have a preview of the
Colossian letter before he delivered it to the church. A better
explanation may be that "ye also" is in contrast to Paul. He
had been discussing the Ephesians' affairs throughout this
letter. Now he says, "You Ephesians may also wish to know
something of my affairs." It was this that Tychicus could
supply.

Paul's concluding benediction included the blessings of
peace, love, faith, and grace. In 1:2 grace and peace were
joined; in 6:23-24 they are separated and named in reverse
order. The "peace" which Paul desires for these Christian
brothers may be explained by his earlier discussions in this

epistle (2:14-17; 4:3). The enjoyment of present tranquillity and spirtual prosperity depends on coming into right relationship with God through Christ, and thus experiencing the unity which the Holy Spirit provides.

The second blessing was "love with faith." This is the love that accompanies true faith because it is the fruit of faith. Thus it is not an undirected sentimentality but the product of regenerated life, received by faith and manifested by love as one of its fruits. For these blessings to abound and be meaningful among them, they must come from "God the Father and the Lord Jesus Christ."

The final blessing is "grace," pronounced on all those who truly love the Lord Jesus Christ. The statement ends with two words which translate literally "in incorruptness." The sense is probably best expressed by the American Standard Version, "them that love our Lord Jesus Christ with a love incorruptible." Surely those whose love for Christ approaches the ideal of that which never decays, never diminishes, and never changes may expect to find the favor (i.e., "grace") of God upon their daily lives in countless and unmistakable ways. Paul found this to be so in his own experience, and he longed for all his readers to share the blessing.

Moody Press, a ministry of the Moody Bible Institute, is designed for education, evangelization and edification. If we may assist you in knowing more about Christ and the Christian life, please write us without obligation to: Moody Press, c/o MLM, Chicago, Illinois 60610.

BIBLIOGRAPHY

Arndt, William F. and Gingrich, F. Wilbur. *A Greek-English Lexicon of the New Testament*. Chicago: U. of Chicago, 1957.

Bruce, F. F. *The Epistle to the Ephesians*. Westwood, N. J.: Revell, 1961.

Eadie, John. *Commentary on the Epistle to the Ephesians*. Grand Rapids: Zondervan, n.d.

Erdman, Charles R. *The Epistle of Paul to the Ephesians*. Philadelphia: Westminster, 1931.

Foulkes, Francis. *The Epistle of Paul to the Ephesians*. Tyndale New Testament Commentaries. Grand Rapids: Eerdmans, 1963.

Gerstner, John H. *The Epistle to the Ephesians*. Shield Bible Study Series. Grand Rapids: Baker, 1958.

Hendriksen, William. *Exposition of Ephesians*. Grand Rapids: Baker, 1967.

Ironside, H. A. *In the Heavenlies*. Neptune, N. J.: Loizeaux, 1937.

Lenski, R. C. H. *The Interpretation of St. Paul's Epistles to the Galatians, to the Ephesians, and to the Philippians*. Columbus, Oh.: Wartburg, 1937.

Martin, Alfred. "The Epistle to the Ephesians." In *Wycliffe Bible Commentary*. Chicago: Moody, 1962.

Martin, W. G. M. "The Epistle to the Ephesians." In *The New Bible Commentary*. Grand Rapids: Eerdmans, 1953.

Salmond, S. D. F. "The Epistle to the Ephesians." In *The Expositor's Greek Testament*, vol. 3. Grand Rapids: Eerdmans, n.d.

Simpson, E. K. *Commentary on the Epistle to the Ephesians*. The New International Commentary on the New Testament. Grand Rapids: Eerdmans, 1957.

Wuest, Kenneth S. *Ephesians and Colossians in the Greek New Testament*. Grand Rapids: Eerdmans, 1953.